T0350644

Hold Open the Door

Hold Open the Door is a fascinating exploration of the meaning of influence and originality. It takes us to the places poetry comes from, places where invisible voices whang and whizz through the air, the wild exchanges between readers, writers, collaborators across the arts. Through the intimacy of formal teaching, the obliquity of the chance encounter, the long-distance correspondence, a poet may find a voice. We encounter the learner's gaze on the model, an exemplar that validates by merely existing; we hear the advice that is resisted until the right moment comes to follow it. The influence may be felt as homage, but it can emerge as a veering away from the model. And then there's the closeness of pastiche. This book shows how various the answers can be, to a single, probing challenge: to show how a beginning poet responds to a model, a teacher, a friend.

Eiléan Ní Chuilleanáin
Professor Emeritus School of English
Trinity College Dublin

What is poetic influence? Who better to answer the question than poets themselves? Responding to the task with magnanimity and insight, the poets assembled here describe those who have given them courage, inspiration, and counsel in ways that no critic could unravel. In prose and verse, critical reflection and poetic meditation, *Hold Open the Door* celebrates the idea of poet as reader and shows how richly rewarding the process of reading can be to the making of poetry.

Philip Coleman
Associate Professor School of English
Trinity College Dublin

John Montague said the ultimate function of the poet is to praise. It's entirely fitting, then, that this book of praise for poets so profoundly and evocatively expresses the tenderness and surprise and complexity experienced by the apprentice in the good light of the master. It's striking and affirming to notice how many of these generous poets and writers are inspired as parents by the works of their mentors. To think the many cherished poets here are already in the imaginative gestures of the newest generation – and therefore in the generation beyond them – is a remarkable thought: the door held open opens not only into other rooms, but into the breath of the century.

Stephen Sexton
School of Arts, English and Languages
Queen's University Belfast

Hold Open the Door

*The Ireland Chair of Poetry
Commemorative Anthology*
2020

Edited by Mícheál McCann, Summer Meline,
Marcella L. A. Prince and Nidhi Zak/Aria Eipe
Advisory Editor: Professor Frank Ormsby

A collaboration between
THE IRELAND CHAIR OF POETRY
and
UNIVERSITY COLLEGE DUBLIN PRESS
Preas Choláiste Ollscoile Bhaile Átha Cliath

First published 2020
UNIVERSITY COLLEGE DUBLIN PRESS
UCD Humanities Institute
Belfield
Dublin 4
Ireland
www.ucdpress.ie

Cover Image: *Ancient Circles* © Iona Howard

ISBN 978-1-910820-75-9

CIP data available from the British Library

The right of Mícheál McCann, Summer Meline, Marcella L. A. Prince and Nidhi Zak/ Aria Eipe to be identified as the editors of this work has been asserted by them

Typeset in Adobe Garamond in Scotland by Ryan Shiels
Printed in Scotland on acid-free paper by Bell & Bain Ltd, Glasgow G46 7UQ, UK

Contents

Foreword

Writers are, first of all, readers. They read in conscious search of those established writers who will excite and ignite them, or in the hope of being ambushed, as it were, by the unexpected, the writer or writers who will 'hold open' and direct them through that partly opened door. The static associations of 'hold', set against the active associations of 'open', function as a balancing device in the title. Its loaded simplicity prompts an engagement we carry into the poems.

The apprentice poets pay tribute on almost every page of this anthology to their poetic enablers. The anthology is itself a substantial tribute, bringing together the students and their mentors, creating new possibilities for encounter and engagement with poetry. The door may open, for example, on the sensitive imitation, the affectionate parody, the exploration of traditional forms and the increasingly assured development of a distinctive voice and a personal style.

Another symbolic door comes to mind, the one Miroslav Holub in his poem 'The door' urges us to open confidently, prepared for both revelation and the attraction of the quotidian:

Go and open the door.
Maybe outside there's
a tree, or a wood,
a garden,
or a magic city…

even if
      nothing
            is there,
go and open the door.

At least
there'll be
a draught.

Frank Ormsby, Ireland Professor of Poetry
OCTOBER 2020

Introduction

On a December evening in Stockholm, Seamus Heaney delivered his acceptance speech for the 1995 Nobel Prize for Literature. 'I credit poetry,' Heaney said, 'both for being itself and for being a help.' Over the course of a remarkably dark and difficult year – the Irish poetic community still mourning the losses of literary luminaries including Ciaran Carson, Eavan Boland and Derek Mahon – *Hold Open the Door* prizes connection within a year that deprived us of it, and reflects on the persisting glow of our mentors, even now.

'Please come flying,' Elizabeth Bishop writes in 'Invitation to Miss Marianne Moore' – the mentor here is invoked to witness what the poet sees, perhaps to see what it is they now write. The younger poet writing to a mentor figure forms as long a tradition as the printed word itself, and this anthology proves that this instinct is strong and sure in Irish writing and beyond. Opening the anthology, James Stafford's poem 'And I Tell Her' echoes with the same cadence as Bishop's, but Stafford forges a playful imaginative mentorship with Elizabeth Bishop where the poem's speaker tells of his observations at the bus stop. 'There are houses there now,' Stafford writes. Here is where the work of this anthology begins. The poems and essays in these pages are not simply humble devotions to important mentors – they spin off in their own surprising ways, now they have the strength in their legs.

For some writers, there is a clear, tangible form of apprenticeship. Paul McMahon tenderly describes how Matthew Sweeney would stab a word on the page when he disagreed with it, only to then beam with 'an endearing smile' when it was suitably resolved. Others note the profound influence that poet-professors have had on their practice, such as Emma Must describing how she travelled by boat from the Isle of Wight to take classes with Mimi Khalvati, or later to Belfast to study under Sinéad Morrissey; or John James Reid recalling that Ciaran Carson, in his weekly Wednesday writers' class, 'broke the surface of my poetic thinking and my resistance to the subject by helping me to see.'

Despite the proliferation of creative writing programmes in the past decades, it is a balm that many writers in this anthology do not necessarily have to be formally taught by a mentor, do not necessarily even have to know them. Perhaps, by deciding to be a writer, you confer your poems to your readers in the knowledge that they may find them instructive. Who are we to tell them otherwise? Rory Duffy, for instance, explains that he has always 'carried an anger' at his early experiences of school, and that Annemarie Ní Churreáin's sustained attention and insight helped him to process those emotions through different angles in his poetry. Sophie Segura notes that, while working as a journalist in Buenos Aires, she was able to 'push back against self-doubt regarding my non-academic path to writing' with the help of Claire Rigby's support. Mentors such as these are breaking down the perception that poetry can only be written by those who are 'qualified' to do so. They are saying, instead: you are human, and you are a *poet*.

While the events of this past year may have served as a stark reminder, it is no secret that poetry is often tasked with saying the unsayable; we turn to it to see us through the harsh winters of our lives. Sometimes, it can even give us the will to live. Evgeny Shtorn speaks of his friendship with Russian poet Galina Gamper, attributing her 'almost-magical capacity to help people stay strong' to helping him endure the darker days. Molly Twomey's unflinching, clear-eyed account of her struggle with an eating disorder outlines the power of the personal connection to a mentor's words and work, and how she comes back – continually – to Leanne O'Sullivan's compassion and wisdom 'when the pain returns, too difficult to numb.'

Mentors can also give us permission to fully inhabit ourselves, as when Nithy Kasa credits Jean O'Brien's oeuvre with encouraging her to embrace her femininity, or when Chandrika Narayanan-Mohan describes how Fióna Bolger's celebration of both her Irish and Indian identities prompted this poet to reclaim aspects of her origin and heritage that she had previously chosen to erase. For Stephen de Búrca, Paul Muldoon's 'formal ingenuity' and 'etymological puns' inspired and 'helped [him] more than most other things to fathom the long, complex tradition of [Ireland's] emigration' as de Búrca himself emigrates from Ireland to the United States.

Elsewhere, two broad columns of the anthology are prose reflections on Eavan Boland and Seamus Heaney, bowing to mentors who were unaware of the seismic importance their presence had on the contributors. In the essay 'Her Knowing', Aoife Lyall reflects on the news of Boland's death in April 2020, and the gift of being seen as a 'mother-poet' by Boland during a brief editorial relationship. '[T]here she was,' Lyall writes, 'holding out a hand, helping me up, letting me get on with it.' In 'The Good Turf', Connie Roberts, having never met Seamus Heaney, cherishes a hand-written note he left for her during a visit to a nondescript Irish bar in Manhattan. 'It is a far, far better thing you do now than you have ever done,' he assures the fledgling poet.

As we celebrate the 25th anniversary year of Heaney's Nobel Award and its legacy, we think back to his own reflections on the value of this mysterious and transformative tradition. Evident in many of his lectures and much of his work over the years – perhaps most unequivocally in his poem 'Fosterage' dedicated to his former Headmaster, Michael McLaverty, where the young protégé finds himself 'newly cubbed in language' – the one that still tugs hardest at the heart is the kinship that he describes feeling for Sweeney, in his introduction to *Sweeney Astray*.

While Heaney remained fascinated – like many who appeal to the literary imagination in Ireland – by the legend of the exiled poet-king, he spoke of his fundamental relationship to Sweeney as being one of place. When he began working on this version of the *Buile Suibhne* poem, he had recently moved to Wicklow, quite close to Sweeney's final resting place at St Mullins. In that 'country of woods and hills, [he] remembered that the green spirit of the hedges embodied in Sweeney' had first been personified for him in one of the members of a local Traveller family, also called Sweeney, whom he would frequently pass camped out in the ditchbacks along the road on the way to his first school. 'One way or another,' Heaney reflects, 'he seemed to have been with me from the start'.

Perhaps this, simply put, is the mentoring relationship: a shared affinity that stays with us from the outset, secret shoulders we are invited to stand upon, the ability to walk farther because those who went before us carved a path. Perhaps, at its heart, it consists of a profound, time-defying friendship – unshakeable, irreplaceable, and 'like most friendships: a little imagined, a little real.'

In these ways, *Hold Open the Door* is, in parts, praise-songs to enduring relationships between mentor and mentee; in others, a created space where a poet pays tribute to a mentor they never knew, but did – somehow – through their work. May the poems and reflections in this anthology be a reminder of this vital practice of connecting with one another and engaging in the generous vulnerability that is writing, reading, and appreciating the poetic impulse. *Hold Open the Door* is a varied and diverse selection of writing that reflects on the sometimes inexplicable yet always revelatory nature of being mentored, and marks an important coordinate on the rich cloth-bound map of Irish poetry to come.

Mícheál McCann, Summer Meline, Marcella L. A. Prince and Nidhi Zak/Aria Eipe
Recipients of the inaugural Ireland Chair of Poetry Student Award
OCTOBER 2020

And I Tell Her

James Stafford

At the bus stop, I tell her
about the market: a yard
for cattle driven up from the station.
There are houses there now,
red brick, narrow,
the name of the estate
on a granite slab
overlaid with paint and marker.

A van has trees for Christmas
and there is a dog
whose owner is nearby.
He can get you cigarettes
and whiskey from the North.

When the newsagent closes,
the children move next door
to hang around the chipper.
Now there is another dog
and they must step over him
under the flashing sign:
a smiling green fish
and red blinking chips.

It is warm inside.
The air is thick.
It is bright and loud and everything moves slowly.
They go in, they order
and they wait. Maybe they eat outside by the door
throwing papers into the overflowing bin,
rolling them tightly so they fall
heavy with grease and salt.

Is this a real place? she asks
and I tell her I was christened
in that church down the street.
It is mostly real, I tell her.
Like most places a little imagined
an imaginary place a little real.

An imaginary mentor; a dialogue with an imaginary friend. When I first read Elizabeth Bishop's 'At the Fishhouses' a decade ago, I let myself into her world. In time, that world moved a little closer to my own and in the narrow red brick houses down by the cattle market pens I could see her 'five fishhouses [with] steeply peaked roofs'. I sent her what started out as a pastiche of that poem set in a Dublin chipper that became a sort of palimpsest where I overwrote her work. Elizabeth called me from time to time (she was particular about her corrections) and our last meeting was at a bus stop on the North Circular Road. Plane trees overhung the place where we talked, green-grey with dust and soot; in her words: 'associating with their shadows'. Most friendships exist discretely in the heads of the two parties, with communication inferred as much as implied, perception standing in for disclosure. My friendship with Elizabeth is like most friendships: a little imagined, a little real.

Daddy Long Legs

Conor Cleary

for Jean Bleakney

Above the hustle of leaves and mulch,
your air-to-earth connection is tenuous,
yet masterful. You willingly play the fool
(stilts and gravitas are at quite the remove)
if it pegs the horizon even slightly further from you.
And then again, in a certain light, don't you seem aloof:
hardly deigning to look down or watch your step,
traversing terrain virtually like something beneath you.
With every grapple-hook stride you seem to imply
that landscape is collapsible in the right frame of mind
and what dictates the difference between scenic and portrait
is less a matter of perspective than of gait.

The first time I read Jean Bleakney's poems I immediately fell in love with their humour, their musicality, and their attention to detail. I particularly admire the scientist's mind at work in her poetry: the microscopic lens that challenges everyday perspectives and rewards us so richly each time we join her in putting our eye to the glass. This is best seen in her many poems that feature plants and insects, to which the above poem is a tribute.

A personal favourite is 'Fenestration' from her collection *Ions*, which colourfully dramatises the plight of winged insects trapped by the invisible barrier of the windowpane. She writes of wasps as a presence,

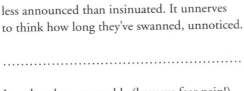

> less announced than insinuated. It unnerves
> to think how long they've swanned, unnoticed.
>
> ....
>
> It makes them amenable (how we fear pain!)
> to the thwack of a Sunday supplement.

Listen to the music in 'long' and 'swanned', the chime between 'unnerves' and 'unnoticed'. By observing the wasp, the speaker also observes their own reaction to it. The tone is both wry and sympathetic, to human and wasp alike. I find myself consistently returning to Bleakney's poems, especially at times when I'm struggling to write. They remind me of what I would like to achieve in my own work: a slant perspective, deft use of sound and images, tenderness and surprise.

The Christmas Orange

Lynn Harding

She was given foreign sunshine
gold bullion, precious ration
of a Blyton childhood
but didn't understand, simply
plucked it, hungry, from his hands and

sank half-moons into a rind
that dug down to tender nail beds.
It was a deeper pain than expected; still
there was the pithy thrill
of flesh as yet untouched.

Above the mantle's stockings
lolled a pomander she did not want.
Dimples in its waxed veneer bled
a tang of oil that tongued the air
with clove, with sex and sandalwood,
tastes she would acquire.

There is still time.

Until then
advent's doors are many
and she knows the way
the wise man knows
to seek a different route.

She had never tasted
pomegranate, but felt its seeds
strain beneath corseted seams.

She cut into the fruit
and found a star to follow.

When I was very young, I read an anthology entitled *Stories for Seven-Year-Olds*. In a chapter which began, 'This is a story of a girl with a name like music, Persephone...' lay my first introduction to a tale that would follow me throughout my life. Later that summer, in a family game of Trivial Pursuit, I was able to proudly answer the question, 'Which fruit did Hades use to capture Persephone?' and fend off accusations of cheating by brandishing my trusty copy of bedtime stories.

I didn't hear the name again until, many years later, Eavan Boland's 'The Pomegranate' introduced me to the layers of subtext and danger that I had missed in my first reading of that timeless myth. By that point a teenager myself, I devoured the story through different eyes, over and over. Now, I was the girl asleep beside the teen magazines and cans of Coke; I was full of unshed tears ready to be diamonds. Even as I felt Boland's angst, I could sense there were things I didn't understand about her experience. It was my first time witnessing the worry of a parent for her growing child without the irritation of it being my own mother, and my first time realising, with black fear, that mine could no more keep the world safe for me than Ceres could for Persephone.

From there, Boland has guided me through my journey as a writer: as a modern poet, a female poet, an Irish poet and a truly practical one, her words have echoed my experiences and given me glimpses of what may come. I had the opportunity to meet her last year, when she selected one of my poems to be published in *Poetry Ireland Review*. I tried to express my gratitude, explain my over-emotional reaction to meeting her; instead, I cried. I like to think she understood.

Her Knowing

Aoife Lyall

It is late on a Sunday evening in July. In the Scottish Highlands, the sun is still out and the bees are steadily making their way through the small field of clover we have left to take over the garden. The children are sleeping in what artificial night we can piece together with black-out curtains and black-out blinds. The effect is more domestic eclipse than deep space: true night will only visit for the hour or two our son wakes for his night feed.

There are trays to be soaked, dishes to be washed, clothes to be dried. There are toys to be cleaned, books to be repaired, bricks and blocks to be re-boxed. Our night will not begin until the day is put right: a night precariously balanced between the need for sleep and the need for company, both conditioned by the vagaries of the baby monitor between us. But, tonight, these things will stay as they are: they have become a still-life I sketch with words. Eavan Boland taught me how to do that, that I could do that. That is her legacy.

I thought this would be easy. But, in truth, I feel like I am back in Junior Infants and drawing a picture for my teacher. I draw with eagerness and purpose and with the nervous pride of knowing she will see it. She may well add a sticker, or perhaps her initials, but neither is as important as her liking it. At four years old, it is my deepest and most singular ambition.

That is how Eavan made me feel. We corresponded several times, in small ways. Two of these exchanges centred on poems she was accepting for publication in *Poetry Ireland Review*. Her first email, a very kind and polite one sent from the States, arrived in the dead of night when I was grappling with a restless baby, a chronic lack of sleep, and a growing sense of a pervasive invisibility settling around me. And then, to have this voice from the other side of the world tell me I had done it, that it had been worth it, that I would be seen: it made me so proud to know – if only for the minutes it took to compose the email – that she had seen me. That she knew something about what I was going through. Two years later, I wrote to her with poems about the inexpressible grief of my miscarriage. When she asked to publish one, I cried: because there she was, holding out a hand, helping me up, letting me get on with it.

Her knowing quelled a fear, let some scar tissue grow, because it was from Eavan I learned to be a mother-poet. Because she was a mother in her poetry. Her children, her private life, were not separate or lesser or discreetly tucked away. From her I learned that someone is a poet first, and then becomes one. That you have to give yourself the authority to write about what is important to you. That motherhood is not some ignoble pursuit, unsuitable for literary interrogation and representation. And so I write, and write about the life around me. When I asked Eavan if she could read my poetry manuscript after it was accepted for publication, her reply was a motherly one: she didn't have the time but wished me all the best.

The picture I paint of Eavan is, of course, an incomplete one, as is the way with any student trying to articulate the significance of a mentor. I did not know her personally, only that I sent her some work that she liked, that she wrote things I agreed with, and those things changed my understanding of, and relationship with, the world and my place in it.

So when I heard the news, I did the only thing I could: I went upstairs and read to my daughter until she fell asleep. I made a point of noticing the soft corduroy of the reading chair, the shouts of still-playing children softened by habit and distance, how her hand got heavier in mine as she fell asleep. I held her hand a little bit longer that night and, watching her sleep, thanked Eavan for what she awoke in me.

A Red Cape for Emily

Monica De Bhailís

I snapped you from the kitchen window – a film
of wavy glass overlays the photo – you're three years old
and already fighting minotaurs in a freezing Narnia.
Intrepid slippers and a flame-red dressing-gown,
wielding the wooden sword you begged for and I made
against my better judgement. Somehow your kit
is your password to open the back of the wardrobe –
my brave girl, I couldn't stop you even if I tried.

Before I knew it, a Great Northern train roared
you away to an Always-Winter – you lit the carriage
with your red, military-style overcoat, but you cried;
on the darkened platform, I was sick as Demeter.
Adventures multiplied, time extended in your wide world
and dangers still intensify, while my life telescopes, races by.
I got good at food parcels but my advice struggles for relevance –
my pomegranate fears, your sparkling nonchalance.

Now I wring my hands in the place where mothers go –
yet wishing for you the best life that you dare,
stillness beyond darkness plumbed, and the horizon
within to meet and mirror your Endless-Elsewhere.
These days we meet on screens – nothing has really changed –

seek out portals for fears and decode wisdoms from the womb.
I still plot your deliverance, long for your returns –
that great scarlet flash when you fly back into *Spare Oom*.

When I first came across Eavan Boland's poetry in the late 1980s, it was a revelation: it seemed like the inner world of my own ordinary experiences was illuminated and elevated into lyric and meaningful moments. In particular, the domestic setting in which I found myself seemed validated and even inspired by her work. When 'The Pomegranate' showed up on the curriculum for my daughter's Leaving Certificate, however, that poem assumed a special significance. For me, the poem conveyed perfectly – both thematically and stylistically – the mother's dilemma in balancing her protective instincts against the wish for her daughter to experience her own, full life – with all its pitfalls and dangers. Reading and discussing the poem became a channel for communicating that ambivalent perspective to my teenage daughter. At the centre of the poem, the pomegranate fruit symbolised everything a mother fears but knows her daughter must experience for herself. The poem, and the myth in which it is framed, included a space for my daughter and I to see our relationship, our differing life-perspectives and the generational *'rifts in time'* between us. Thus, the poem's theme of myth as representing common ground for understanding universal experiences became embodied in our story. When my now-adult daughter found inspiration for courage in a photo of herself as a child at play in her own, imagined underworld of Narnia, it brought that process into focus for me again, transforming an ordinary mother's wish for her daughter into a poem: 'A Red Cape for Emily'.

Kala Pani

Chandrika Narayanan-Mohan

Kala Pani means 'black water' in Hindi and is referenced in Fióna Bolger's poem 'Mary and Sunil.' She explains that 'it is believed by some that crossing the sea erased caste and community ties.'

When I met Fióna Bolger five years ago, she was excited to learn that I was from India. It had been almost two decades since I'd left the country, and I didn't really know how to talk about my old life, or myself, within the context of 'Indian-ness'. I didn't understand why she had to be so curious about me, and the part of my life I considered ancient history. What was important was my life here, in Ireland. Wasn't my carefully-crafted Irish persona enough?

When I read *a compound of words*, I understood why it wasn't enough. In her collection, Fióna binds, wraps, and stitches together her absorption into Indian culture, her drives on the East Coast Road, her relationship with a spice shelf, and the way she offers that life up to her Indian-Irish daughter. Her poems swoop and dive behind the eyes of Indian people that blink into her life – from the woman cutting coconuts on the street in 'The Coconut Seller' to the steel magnates that dominate the Indian newspapers in 'Lakshmi Mittal in Zenica'. Through that special clarity that poetry provides, she addresses her complicated cultural background and mixed national identity. She has done what I have been unable to do.

I am Indian, but I don't generally connect to my nationality as part of my identity. I am the daughter of a diplomat and a World Bank employee, and granddaughter of the former President of India. The cities I've called home are New Delhi, Washington, D.C., Stockholm, Ankara, York, London, and Dublin. As a third culture kid, I have a complicated relationship with the idea of home and national identity.

When I lived in India, I always felt like a bit of a foreigner and never quite fit in. Traveling with my Ambassador mother, I was used to being in international schools with all the other kids whose lives hovered between countries. Being an immigrant, I used my diplobrat talents to assimilate and shed my former life over and over again, always congratulating myself on my ability to absorb the accent as quickly as possible, and be mistaken for a local, despite the colour of my skin.

So when I kept running into Fióna at literary events, I panicked as she kept trying to talk to me about India. I would freeze up, not knowing how to relate to an Irish person who was obviously more 'Indian' than I could ever be. She encouraged me to attend events, to be a part of the Indian community in Ireland, but my instinct was to run a mile. My experience of Indian communities has always been mixed: people would be my friends until they realised I was not going to commit to their Indian-only social group, or they would judge me – with snide comments – for not speaking fluent Hindi. Heaven forbid they found out who my grandfather was, because then I would seem like even more of a disgrace. So, faced with encountering all my cultural insecurities, I tried to politely decline Fióna's invitations.

But Fióna doesn't tend to give up so easily. I was introduced gradually to some of the people in her circle, and tentatively realised I could happily get along with them. Maybe I'd even laugh at an Indian in-joke that I would find myself understanding. I realised that I was not the anomaly in these circles: I was the norm. Most of these people were of South-East Asian origin, who also had a mixed idea of what home was, and were passionate about writing and literature. Over the years Fióna has given me a platform, personal support, and inspiration, while connecting me to many brilliant writers I would not have known without her. She has been a creative collaborator, a mentor, and a friend. In the world I had whitewashed for myself in order to fit in, she provided a bridge back to my former life that, until now, I've been too scared to cross.

Fióna's work made me realise that we are two sides of the same coin: she is Irish with deep connections to India, and I am Indian with deep connections to Ireland. We both struggle with coming to terms with our countries of origin, and have both fallen uncontrollably and deeply in love with somewhere else, where we have tasted belonging – where something felt *right*. However, these are also places where our unbelonging shines out through our skin, our voices, and the ways we move through the world. I have only written about my adopted home, and of my unbelonging, always making sure to be palatable to my mostly white Irish audience. Fióna weaves this journey of multiple homes through her writing, unapologetically making references that an Irish audience won't understand.

But now, ignited by the words in her poems, I feel I am on the precipice of finally looking back. Words like:

| Doodh walla | Dhobi | Rasam | Idli | Diyas |

| Jeera | Saunf | Tabla | Chowkidar | Pani |

| Raga | Ek do theen | Chinni | Brinjal | Fevicol |

… words that are like sparks lighting the dark as my eyes fall upon them. When she talks about banana leaves, I am at a South Indian autumn festival, stuffing my face with parippu and papad, while hoping nobody sees how bad I am at eating with my hands. When she mentions mishti doi, I remember the feeling of a cool terracotta pot straight out of the fridge filled with a creamy, slightly sour curd that stuck to the sides, that I could have eaten buckets of. When she mentions the newscaster in her yellow sari, I can hear the blare of the NDTV news channel that always jars me. I *get it*, these words and phrases and references, and it is a rare feeling to have a secret insight into something that my Irish friends don't. I am so used to being on the outside looking in, that the feeling of being in on the joke is alien and disconcerting.

I have fought against thinking and writing about my memories of India for a number of reasons: unprocessed grief, lack of closure, cultural insecurities, and the parts of Indian culture and society that have hurt me and my family. But I also didn't write about these experiences because they are contained within the life I was dealt, not the life I have built. Because of a life dictated by family, or immigration policies, I didn't like thinking about the life I didn't have control over. I revelled in being known for my love letters to Dublin, for my poems about mental health and immigration, but poems about being Indian? No. I didn't want to play into people's expectations of the brown girl in front of the microphone. I chose to prove them wrong by erasing myself. I refused to perform as my former self.

But the past has a way of seeping through. When I was in New Delhi last year, I felt my brain formulate a poem. My mother and I were walking along a path, and the ground was covered in a particular red, gritty, sandy gravel that covers many walking areas in the city. For the first time, I really listened to the grind of it underfoot, to the shuffle of it, inhaled the warm sandstone-dust smell of it. And I was on the verge of committing it to paper, but something in my head stopped me. Writing about India felt like pushing the same poles of a magnet together: the harder I pushed, the stronger the repulsion.

In the end, I didn't write the poem. But after reading *a compound of words* not once, but three times, I can feel the cracks forming, and my muscles loosening, and the past leaking in. Fióna's words have unlocked the memories I have shoved aside, and I can finally feel them bubbling into shapes that I can form, and type, and print. This essay is the first time I have ever addressed these issues in writing, and it will not be the last. Thanks to her, the poems are on their way.

Stranger

Milena Williamson

Walking farther than I've been before brings me to Tomb Street.
I'm a stone's throw away from Royal Mail, but I don't know where

and it's early days in Belfast and I've not got mail from anyone.
It's as good a street as any for learning how to look left and listen—

how's tricks catch yerself on aye meet yous at the back of Boots
I'll run ye over sure I almost lost the run of myself lookin at him.

I'm stood there searching for something déjà vu.
To feel like I've been before in a place I've never been

is all I can ask of this here city built on *wait until the green man*
shows opposite the north is next to let give way no ball games.

Feeling grows familiar as I peel a tangerine to smithereens.
I turn again into Tomb Street— *private gate keep clear*

queue here at any time on footway no persons beyond this point.
The inner ring does my head in as I follow it round and exit too early.

I call my father across the ocean and say *bout ye* are you there
ach sure ye know yerself can you hear me *right I'm away home.*

The first time I attended a poetry workshop with Ciaran Carson, he asked what I thought of a peer's poem. I admitted that because there were so many Northern Irish words in the poem, I didn't actually know what was happening. Three years later, I'm still studying poetry in Belfast. My comprehension of Northern Irish-English is always evolving, never complete. That day, Ciaran invited me into the Northern Irish literary community. He taught me that my unfamiliarity with Northern Irish words simply meant I had an opportunity to learn, to play with language, to develop my poetry in a cultural context different to the one I grew up in. Ciaran's poetry was my map to Belfast; in 'Turn Again', if even the most familiar inhabitants of Belfast have to 'think again' to find their way, then surely I could accept being a little lost as a newcomer.

Ciaran's poems helped me appreciate both Belfast and my hometown of Swarthmore, Pennsylvania. I have a deep knowledge of Swarthmore that I carry with me; it is the only place where 'when someone asks me where I live, I remember where I used to live.' And yet, the longer I spend in Belfast, the more this here city becomes my adult home and my poetic home. I learn the vernacular of place – Tomb Street, the Inner Ring, the back of Boots – names which find their way into my poem. As Ciaran writes in the poem 'Turn Again', these streets are my 'Ireland's Entry'. And as long as I live in Belfast, much like the speaker in Ciaran's 'Queen's Gambit', I will search for that 'something déjà vu'.

Entries

John James Reid

Brick-lined or lime-washed
corridors for conversations,
with coal men and bin men, play spaces
for children, love spaces for first feels
and first kisses, spaces of entrapment
for bullies and beatings, knee cappings,
escape tunnels from the boys and soldiers,
empty mostly, but alive with invisible breath.

The memory of him recurs to this day,
crouched, an automatic rifle across his knees,
bottom of the entry after school. *Go home kid.*
I remember seeing him again in the Kitchen Bar,
many years later, at Christmas,
amidst the music, the crackle of the fire.

I attended Ciaran Carson's Wednesday writers' class at the Seamus Heaney Centre in Belfast, after some success at poetry summer schools, and forwarding some early unpublished pamphlets to him. I am an architect. Ciaran suggested that I write about architecture. This might seem obvious in some ways, but it was not to me – why would I want to write about glorified architecture that had already been written about?

Ciaran encouraged me to consider its unique language and its potential. He broke the surface of my poetic thinking and my resistance to the subject by helping me to see – not the architecture of grandness, but the architecture of something else. I re-discovered the humble Belfast clay brick; its warm peach colour, its decorative detail, and its rich history. I found words, poetry and memory in clay.

Ciaran's mentoring set me on a journey of creative self-reflection, through poems about the terrace house I was born in, the entries I played in, and the memories of those brick spaces: their history and violence through the Troubles. The 'magical bricks' of the Pharaohs. A man who was killed by a brick in the riots. The humble brickbox used across centuries of manufacture from the earth and human endeavour. Ciaran Carson was the architect of this idea in me. It was a creative idea, that mushroomed into a Belfast idea and expanded into a lovely search in bricks and words. It's a Belfast story reaching into itself, into language and a smaller world, and has been the mentoring experience of my life.

With the Key Still in Your Pocket

David Morgan O'Connor

Built to dissuade protest or jumping, an example of how the Irish do
brutal Bauhaus, rain every Wednesday on campus all autumn we shuffle

into the dank room. Wet and slouching to riff and joust but mostly listen to the history
of Irish literary journals by drinking from the fountain. The sun sets earlier each week

we all notice but no one comments because awe is a cast spell and hypnosis
a gift only ears can hook the gems of phrase buffered to share why else

would anyone cross these empty and altered landscapes? She lifts her mind off the wheel.
Eyes close, the bridge all suspension, detour warning slipped past unnoticed.

Was it Romania or Rome we were headed? Passing round an orange, big as a road map,
Kavanagh's Weekly; The Story of An Editor Who Was Corrupted by Love.

And I'm rolling all over the backseat of this fluent pantry, my clown wig floored,
this shifting realm takes flight, covers turn wings, the room regresses to childhood

when generous aunties spoiled and treated and brothers and mothers lived and teased
and helped sound out the big words by chiselling accent—where is my copy   I think

in a box in a garage attic under a snowbank, used as kindling, sold to feed the gas meter?
Dense magic, a necessary jolt always asking, rarely answering.

Put a nun on a train. Ride through a tunnel. Awake in a flood. Cobwebs on eyelash.
Exit hard to find. Time is translated and divided then gone. It's winter, no brakes.

Near Seafort Parade in Blackrock Park, the reverent daffodils bow.

When I think of mentors, I don't know where to begin or end. There have
been so many – I've been very lucky. I am grateful. But I'll never forget
being in a dull institutional room, J208 at University College Dublin to be
precise, listening to Eiléan Ní Chuilleanáin riffing and counterpointing
on the history of Irish literary journals, language, writing, and translation.
I felt that rare and glorious sensation, in lightning-fast waves, that we were
speaking a shorthand – the summations of thousands of private hours
reading and playing word-games, as readers, writers, and students must.

As if on command, the rain would obscure the sunlight, if there was
any; and a remark, reference, observation, and always Eiléan's questions –
would open a door to a view, a memory, which would make this practice
of reading and writing feel worthier than food. One session, Eiléan
brought in her copy of *Kavanagh's Weekly,* the exact same issue my aunt, a
nun in Dundalk, had sent me as a gift in Canada in the mid 1980s. I was
far too young to understand the journal but I loved having a copy; and
holding it again brought a tiny epiphany – isn't writing all about sharing?

Eiléan's words helped me through that winter. This poem, like others,
contains those allusions and nods – the nun on the train, the bridge, the
key and the pocket. Her encyclopaedic wisdom and honest style continues
to inform and interlace with my work. She is a true and generous master.

A Lake Dweller's Death

Rory Duffy

Slowly the oars are tucked into the grasp of
the skinny-finger water.
They dip their spade-heads,
scratching at the jagged bed
like sleepless teeth.
Out from the shore the dry leather saddles
begin to creak their mummified song
until an arthritic hand scoops water and salves their cries.
As the beat begins, the heron-grey water
presses itself through the staves
and into the white shirt sleeves
of two strong forearms.
We move, humming with the strum
of the lake's throbbing heart,
its ripple beat rattles at our black-trousered seats.
From the pocked edge
we push his final journey,
slipping across the skin of the lake.
The knife of the keel splits it
like the crack of a steel blade
on dry flotsam wood.
It unzips the watery veneer
into Westmeath and Roscommon,
Leinster and Connaught.
We pass Whinnion, the Long Shoal

and the Cribbys before brushing
into the shelter of the reedy bay.
As a westerly breeze begins to pick
the white tops off the slate waves
we move gently towards the other side,
grinding hull-wood announcing
our message to step ashore.
We snake up the hillside
towards the lean of the cemetery,
shouldering the teak of his hard-work body
until we stand by the open grave.
As the sun begins to cut into the crimson horizon
we watch, breathless and fire handed,
as his final berth begins.

Having only gained the courage to write in my late forties, I eventually succumbed to poetry when over fifty. I left school without a Leaving Cert in 1981 following a horrendous experience in schooling. In 2019, I was fortunate to be selected for the John Broderick Mentorship scheme in Athlone. I therefore got to spend time with Annemarie Ní Churreáin, looking at poetry and my own writing. Her approach had a profound effect on me. I witnessed her total dedication to the power of each word in each sentence and how the themes that run through work need to be teased and pulled until they revealed themselves. 'The Secret' from *Bloodroot* showed me this clearly. This was a moment when my understanding of poetry turned and I saw the power of words in healing and moving forward. I have always carried an anger at my early experiences of school and saw this as a root cause of my need to write. However, I learned that I was dealing with this issue too directly. I needed to let this issue speak openly through other words and angles. I saw how this energy could be allowed to go in other directions and express itself through beauty as well as anger, through soft as well as hard words. My poem is a positive inversion of that chaos and I am indebted to Annemarie for these revelations.

The Crossing Hour

Julie Morrissy

after Harry Clifton

Late on weekend nights, after we had bungled
Back up Wexford Street, slid through the door and over
Bikes in the hallway, chips hot in our hands,
The voices would come. Booming outside
Our first-floor window, sing-song and stuttering,
Like their footsteps towards the taxi-dream
Of Rathmines. Inside, two adults let free, our days filled
With each other, as we doubled our wardrobes. The voices
Outside steady throughout, sometimes mingled with
Our own – somewhere on South Richmond Street, I left my outdoor
Voice. Maybe locked in 57 or on the steps of 58, it's hard to
Remember – we have been pushed from the canal, wardrobes
Too far now to swap clothes. I don't walk by the house
Late at night anymore. But if I did, it would be whispers.

I first met Harry Clifton in 2013 during my Master's degree in Creative Writing, while he was based at University College Dublin as Ireland Professor of Poetry. Harry led a class in which students sat together and read poetry aloud from across the ages. I have since kept up this practice of reading out loud to myself, with other people's work and when I am drafting my own poems. At that point I had just begun writing poetry seriously and I had yet to publish a poem. In the following years Harry and I ended up as neighbours in Portobello, living just a few streets apart. I frequently ran into him and we would often go for a pint. Our friendship has been an important source of encouragement for me. He treats me as his peer, and his generous spirit is well-known in the poetry community. Harry's recent collection, *Portobello Sonnets*, offers a lightness and curiosity that strike me as particularly characteristic of that area of Dublin. There was a time when everyone I knew lived in Portobello and it seemed like the centre of the universe. I don't live there anymore, but Harry's book transports me back to a time and a place that is very dear to me. And so, I took some time to sit by the canal and write my own Portobello sonnet, inspired by that place 'Between night and morning' in his sonnet '32'.

Learning Prose from the Poet

Peter Frankman

I first met Harry Clifton at a welcome luncheon at Trinity. He was a lean man in a green sweater, a sweater I'd soon recognise as a staple of Harry's wardrobe – so worn it was translucent at the edges and dangled from his limbs. He smiled readily as his new pupils approached him. After a bit of small talk, I told him why I'd come to study in Ireland: I needed to know if I could write 'for real'. I figured if I gave myself a solid year of writing under experienced professors without the distractions of home, I might be able to determine if I could make it as a writer. It was a last-ditch sort of effort; if I wasn't talented enough or couldn't work things out, I'd focus on another career path.

During this first meeting, I called him 'Professor Clifton', something that made him wince.

"Harry's fine," he told me. He also assured me we'd figure out if I could write before the year was over.

There was a question in my mind of how Harry's teaching would translate to me, given that Harry is a poet and I was attempting to write a novel. I felt myself confronted with a potential waste of four months. I suspected Harry might focus his attention on the students in our course dedicated to poetry, leaving me to figure things out on my own. Either that or his lessons might revolve around flowery details and lovely language.

Specifically, I worried a poet would lose track of the bigger picture of the novel I was writing. I was nervous Harry might not have much experience in writing or editing dialogue, a large part of my writing. I thought we might get caught up trying to make one single paragraph *perfect* – the kind of perfect a poet can afford to look for in 14 lines of a sonnet, but I wasn't ready to pursue in my 80,000 word story about a hamster.

However, I soon found all my fears were unfounded.

Words flowed easily from Harry. His advice for my writing often came by comparing it to writers I'd never heard of, but soon came to admire – Isaac Bashevis Singer, Tim Winton, and others. Although Harry challenged me immensely, his instruction came from a place of positivity and optimism. He would ask about things I'd never thought of asking myself: questions about the socioeconomic standing of characters, how the setting reflected the tone, and what each word I chose contributed not only to the sentence it was in, but to the chapter and book as a whole. I soon understood his philosophy was to be clear, concise, and complete.

I waited until after taking Harry's class to read his writing. This wasn't anything personal about him – I was always afraid I'd be influenced by reading someone's work before taking their class. I worried I'd either try writing too much like the instructor or maybe I wouldn't like their writing and – consciously or subconsciously – I'd pay less attention to what they had to say.

Then I read Harry's writing and I enjoyed it. I liked his poetry, all of which felt nearly timeless in subject-matter and style. His work stands in stark contrast to my own writing, which is rooted in contemporary life and culture. However much I enjoyed his poetry, I was apprehensively drawn to his memoir, *On the Spine of Italy: A Year in the Abruzzi*. My fear was a book of prose by a poet might be long-winded and overwrought; I expected a terrible slog. Once again, my assumptions were wrong. I didn't just like the book: I *loved* it.

On the Spine of Italy recounts the year Harry and his wife, Deirdre, spent in a remote village in the Italian mountains. Throughout the memoir there are few significant events moving the story along. Instead of bouncing from one action-packed scene to the next, the reader experiences the humdrum nature of life in this remote culture – yet it is a captivating read. For me, every detail of the tiny village felt clear and every character felt familiar after their first appearance. Soon I realised what worked so well in the book was the combination of Harry's poetic mind and the fact he was following the same rules he'd taught me all year. He relied on an economy of words to tell his story, painted clear pictures of the setting without becoming convoluted, and he moved through the consciousness of his own narration to the action of the scene seamlessly.

I finished reading Harry's book in the summer, when he and I would meet regularly at Bewley's Café to review my writing. I'd known Harry during one of the most turbulent years of my life – one in which I'd made and lost friends, finished the first draft of a novel I'd been plotting for months beforehand, and decided what I wanted to do for the rest of my life. Through it all, Harry remained unchanged. Though my innate anxiety would have me arrive ten or 15 minutes early, Harry would already be there. He liked sitting in the back section, away from the busy kitchen, in an effort to avoid the wait staff and patrons buzzing about. From a distance, I watched the poet. Harry, wearing the same green sweater even on the hottest of summer days, with his cuppa to the right, a pen in his hand, and a notebook out before him. He was always totally engrossed in his work.

When I would sit down across from Harry, I felt complete tranquillity, focusing only on the discussion at hand. Harry was concerned about me in a genuine, decent way. He would encourage me to get a coffee and eat something in front of him, as if he didn't believe I was eating on my own. We would talk about our lives a bit, which usually meant me telling Harry about the jobs I'd been applying for and where I might live when the program ended.

"You'll be fine." Harry addressed my concerns in a simple, confident manner. He recommended working as a part of society and writing as a necessary part of my life. He wasn't saying this to placate my concerns or move the conversation along – that wasn't his way. Harry truly believed in my ability as a writer.

"I liked your book," I told him. "*On the Spine of Italy*, I mean."

Harry looked surprised – as if it was the first time he'd heard of his own memoir. He thanked me, of course, but quickly moved us along to discussing edits he wanted to suggest for my work. I didn't bring up his memoir again, but I smiled when we talked about making the location of my story more of a character than simply the setting, keeping my word choice concise, and defining characters in only a sentence or two – those exact details the poet had captured so perfectly in his own prose.

Though it has been over a year since I left Ireland, I often think back on the lessons Harry taught. Instead of rushing to fit all my ideas onto the page in some slapdash fashion, I take my time and choose my words carefully. When editing my writing, I think about being clear, concise, and complete. I consider whether a reader would enjoy the atmosphere of what I'm writing in the same way I enjoyed reading *On the Spine of Italy*. More than anything, I think about the deliberate way in which Harry acts. And the quiet confidence with which he carries himself. There's no reason to rush.

The view from Dun Laoghaire

Ruth Kelly

The click of the crochet hook becomes a habit.
Doilies stretch like spiders' webs
Across every surface, gathering dust.
The try-harder generations stand before us,
A bunch of run-aways and zealots,
And curse us for our terrible wings.
The country's taken to spinning nettles
To turn our wings to arms to work the land
Courting swollen fingers and foreign cash.
Men and women born to spend and trade
In greasy envelopes and fiscal settlements
And painted facades all the length of that parade.
The clink of glasses. Headlights glitter in the mist.
Spinning and spinning and holding things still.
Wild swans and wild geese wheel overhead
Beating and clipping the wind and the rain.
We were rich once and might be again.
Bury me at Tara when my wings are torn away.

The title nods to Nuala Ní Dhomhnaill's 'Radharc Ó gChabhán tSíle': an uneventful suburban evening's viewing of news reports of bombing 'ar bhruachbhailte mar seo.' Standing instead overlooking Dun Laoghaire harbour, I pick up on lines from 'September 1913' that have stuck with me since school, and on Yeats' likely distaste for people like me in his vision of romantic Ireland. Ní Dhomhnaill's old Ireland is a darker, more sensual place, and her recuperation of myth something more manic, set oddly but believably against the day-to-day. Her work brings together the tug of home and of the past with the impulse to leave, to run away. Figuring my way through the Irish, I am struck by the range of theme and style, by the way ancient Greece and old Ireland are often intertwined, and often by her controlled use of metre and rhyme. Ní Dhomhnaill's expression of femininity spans day-to-day detail, the possibility of confident and satisfied sexuality, philosophical reflections, and the experience of being overwhelmed. Writing in Irish I am caught up; it is a revealing and not entirely controlled process that brings out unexpected focus and is structured by rhythms and half-remembered words that turn out, when I look them up, to be oddly precise. Writing in English, I want to have access to that range, to borrow from the past in ways that take account of older and more recent traditions about what we can and cannot do, but remake them.

Teacht Slán

Joanne McCarthy

Beireann crogaill uibheacha, UIBHEACHA!
a scairteann amach an leaid is óige,
a mhalaí chomh ardaithe
nach féidir liom focal a rá dó
faoi *Steigí* an dineasár ag geonaíl
go deo sa seomra breagáin

nó an tslí nach mactíre aonarach í an ghealach,
go bhfuil deirfúireacha aici ar fud na réaltraí,
col ceathracha ina réaltbhuíonta
col seisreacha ina dreigíte

Conas go insoed dó faoin Chicxulub Impactor,
an coilíneach sin, ar mharaigh muintir Steigí uilig?

Conas go dtagann said amach slán as an mblaosc a mham?
Le fiacla beaga géara a fhreagraím.
Agus.
Raghaimid lá go Meicsiceo, tá poll sa talamh ann.
Chaithfinn é a thaispeáint duit.

Safe Landing

Crocodiles lay eggs, EGGS!
the youngest lad cries,
his eyebrows raised so high
I can't say a word about the origin
of Steigí, the dinosaur who groans
all day in the toy room

nor can I tell the moon is no lone wolf,
she has kin all over the galaxy,
constellation cousins
and meteorite sisters

because how could I speak
about the Chicxulub Impactor,
that black sheep,
who murdered Steigí's kind?

How do they come out of the eggs, mam?
With sharp little teeth, I answer.
And.
Some day we'll go to Mexico.
There's a hole in the ground waiting for you.

I was a student in University College Cork the first time I read *The Astrakhan Cloak*, and the work had a powerful effect on me. Twenty years later, I still go back to these poems regularly, so much so that some – such as 'The Crack in the Stairs', 'First Communion Day' and 'I Fall in Love' – are like close friends. I love Ní Dhomhnaill's use of imagery and the way she weaves the magical and the grit of the real through her work; like when she writes that she falls in love –

> le gach a bhfuil ag dul as:
> Leis na prátaí ag dubhadh is ag lobhadh istigh sa chlais
> Leis na Brussels sprouts ag meirgiú ar an gais
> Ruaite ag an mbleist seaca, searbh is tais

> with all that's going off:
> with blackened spuds rotting in their beds, with
> Brussels sprouts nipped in the bud
> by a blast of frost, rat-eaten artichokes

When Ní Dhomhnaill says that her children, when young, were muses for her, she gives me space and permission to allow my children to influence me and my writing. In 'Aubade', for instance, Ní Dhomhnaill opens up the love poem to make space for children. The lovers face the day so 'Our children can drink water from broken bowls / Not from cupped hands.' Everything in this poem speaks to me as a mother of young children who 'has to make do with today's happenings.'

Between image, sound, rhythm and her richness and mastery of language, Ní Dhomhnaill never fails to take me by the hand and lead me somewhere special.

Sonic

Matthew Rice

for Ian Duhig

1991: a submerged maze
of ancient ruins
off South Island's prominent range —
my past lives are littered there,

oxygen bubbles glimpsed like UFOs.
Your way with the controller, more finger
than thumb: forward-forward-down-A,
turbo-roll, cannonball.

You are levels above.
The scenery repeats-repeats,
a hidden switch must be found.
Star Light — Spring Yard — Green Hill,

the years light on their feet;
I mimic your patient hands.

In the summer of 1991, I was ten years old. Around this time, the video game *Sonic the Hedgehog* had been released on the Sega Megadrive. Like many children of my generation, I was captivated by the new titles that were being produced by Sega. Sonic was by far my favourite, however. I would play for hours, and if I was stuck on a level, I would make it my day's mission to conquer it.

During this period, another video game enthusiast entered my life. His name was Ian Duhig. He and my father, Adrian, had become close friends over the previous couple of years due to their mutual status as emerging poets. Ian had recently won the UK National Poetry Competition, and my father had, the year before, published his first poems to reputable acclaim. I was aware of the creative atmosphere around me. However, it was when Ian stayed at our house in Islandmagee, County Antrim, in the summer of '91 that I first appreciated his prodigious talent: he completed *Sonic the Hedgehog* in a single afternoon.

In the years since, Ian has been a constant source of encouragement, offering invaluable and innumerable levels of feedback on my own work. He has often been one of the first readers of manuscript drafts, and in particular has offered advice on my upcoming debut collection, for which I will be forever grateful. His attitude keeps me grounded, summed up in a recent email response to a poem of mine when he referenced Bede's sparrow flying quickly through the hall. 'Which is all life is.'

The Well

Peggy McCarthy

We lean in low with secrets to tell
to the still cold water and the briary stone.
Haul up the bucket from the darkened well.

Cast down to a place below the swell
of sodden clay and waters unknown.
We lean in low with secrets to tell.

Was it here we threw coins to dispel
the lurk of dark shadow lodged moons ago?
Heave up the bucket from the gaping well.

Silent ripples flatline and circle
outreaching the touch of time and bone.
We lean in low with secrets to tell.

Childlike wishes and prayers impelled
the water to hold us and endlessly flow.
Hoist up the bucket from the sunless well.

Searching now to reclaim and retell
stories run dry and long overgrown.
We lean in low with secrets to tell.
Haul up the bucket from the darkened well.

Paul Durcan is a poet I've loved throughout the years. Since I first heard him reading in Waterford back in 1993 from *A Snail in My Prime: New and Selected Poems*, I was hooked. His voice was alive and enthralling. I still treasure my signed copy of this collection, while *Life is a Dream* is always within reach at my desk!

I witnessed the powerful effect of refrain in poetry read so entrancingly by Durcan himself that evening in 1993. Those repeated lines lodged and have beguiled me ever since: 'Oh but it's the small bit of furze between two towns / Is what makes the Kilfenora teaboy really run' ('The Kilfenora Teaboy') or 'Making love outside Aras an Uachtaráin' in the poem by the same name.

In writing 'The Well', the villanelle form lends itself to that movement of the repeated line as a kind of thread that recedes, rounds and returns throughout the poem. I'm intrigued by the sound and that sense of circling back.

I strive for that lightness of touch in Durcan's poems whether he's addressing public or deeply personal themes. His oblique approach and unique comic spirit are evident even in poem titles. Who wouldn't crack a smile at 'The Man with a Bit of Jizz in Him', 'The Woman Who Keeps Her Breasts in the Back Garden', 'The Married Man Who Fell in Love with a Semi-State Body', or 'The Head Transplant'? – titles that belie searing truths.

His work inspires and sustains me.

Spacelessness

Evgeny Shtorn

to Galina Gamper, in memoriam

If you want to break out
to make your own way
if you crave the light
from the kingdom of shadows
you need to leave yours behind
forget forever
bid farewell
and never remember

Then in a thousand Fridays
through endless time
severe freezing in zero gravity
leaning on a smartphone-crutch
you will conquer plaintively

Let me return to that
spacelessness
with the facades peeled off
where instead of green grass
only frost dust lay
my shadows were flat there

in long-awaited graves
they knew how to hurt me
like no one ever could
let me let me let me
forgiving each other
is unnecessary

A dusty cloud parts
in silence as a sea
and you will find a way home

Беспространство

Памяти Галины Гампер

Если ты вырваться хочешь
если ты хочешь пробраться
если ты жаждешь
из королевства теней
то тень свою нужно оставить
забыть навсегда
распрощаться и не вспоминать

Потом через тысячу пятниц
через бесконечное время
застыв в невесомости тяжкой
на костыле из смартфона
завоешь ты жалобно·

Дайте
вернуться мне в то беспространство
туда где фасады облезли
и вместо травы зеленящей
заиндевелая пыль
там тени мои распластались
в своих долгожданных могилах
там те кто обидеть умели
как никогда и никто
позвольте позвольте позвольте
прощать нам друг друга не нужно

Пыльное облако молча
расступится что твое море
и ты возвернешься домой.

Galina Gamper (1938-2015) was a Russian poet, and my only formal mentor of poetry. I attended her literary seminar from 2012 to 2014. I also visited her in the Writers' Residency in Komarovo, near Petersburg. Komarovo became famous among Russian poets because Anna Akhmatova spent her last summers and was buried there.

I met Gamper during one of the most difficult periods of my life, when I had become a stateless person. There is no room here to go into the details, but her care and attention helped me to survive those dark days. I attribute her almost-magical capacity to help people stay strong to her own life experience. Since early childhood, Gamper had been confined to a wheelchair. She had an extremely difficult life, but her vitality, optimism, kindness and passion for poetry was a salvation for me, and many others around her.

She describes pain, desperation, and loneliness as reasons for existence – seeing them not only as meaningful, but also as interesting and attractive emotions and experiences. She always reflected on the unknown force that gave her life, rather than complaining about her destiny. For her, optimism was synonymous with courage, and this informed her writing. Her poem 'Krutaya Lestnitsa' that can be translated as 'Jacob's Ladder' particularly resonates with me and is the inspiration for the poem I wrote. She writes:

> Downed, what will give you support
> without letting mind and gaze fade away?
> How can you resist?
> But you certainly will resist.

This poem in memory of Galina Gamper – initially written in Russian – forms part of the manuscript of my first collection, *Translating from Myself.* I am trying to follow her path, in describing home as a place of suffering, of frozen dust, but still a place to come back to.

Elegy for the Steel Workers

Sven Kretzschmar

after Francis Harvey

White-burning fire-snakes hiss
out of the darkness into the half-gloom
of the rolling mill. The workers barely blink.

Dark fumes hang under a concrete factory ceiling,
smell of sinter, steel dust and sweat evaporates.
On slow shifts they swap trivia, toil, wait

for the changeover. Drink and smoke harden
them and when they talk, it is harsh,
with a coarse humour about those who went

through the factory gate, those on whom
the umbrage of the hillsides fell.
Their hardship is penned in heat and shadow;

some hardly live to see their pension
and on their deathbed remember the line
someone engraved on a dirty girder:

Only the dead are out of their element.

In 'Elegy for the Steel Workers', I draw on the work of Francis Harvey, particularly on some poems from his 1978 collection *In the Light on the Stones*. I come from a rural background, so, even though I never met Harvey, and spent most of my time in Ireland living in Dublin, his poetry about landscape and nature made a strong, lasting impression on me. In many of his poems, Harvey describes the hardship of life in Donegal, between granite hills and the Atlantic, and the old and dwindling jobs there like that of the drover or the cowherd. He writes with a sober voice, with a grounded distance to his objects – there is a compassionate practicality in his words. It strikes a chord with me as a trained analytic philosopher and, in my own writing, I often find myself returning to Harvey's work to seek inspiration. In writing this poem, I thought about how his compassionate practicality could be carried over to my native Saarland, Germany, and its traditional professions. It is a landscape shaped by agriculture, but also by coal mines and steel plants. Since I was a steel worker during semester breaks, I decided to write about a local steel mill. The Harvey poems I drew on are 'Elegy for the Islanders', 'Condy', 'Elegy for a Robin' (from which the last line of my poem was taken); they can be found in Harvey's *Collected Poems*, published by Dedalus Press.

The Sawmill

Marguerite Doyle

In the brittle heat of summer, sudden lightning
brings us like thieves to pick over leavings.
Scaling the chain link fence of rusted diamonds —
cutting knuckles, scraping elbow, knee.
He clacks across his labours; sun bleached bones,
slap of stack and ochre butcher's dust.
At each cut another woodland cloud
spurts in the rude glare of August.
The shrill *birr* and *wirr* of toothed blade —
cut-offs plunge in deep pile. Time cleaves,
the saw cuts out, and at the siren's wail
he winks into silence and his tea.
Our chance for hurlies, flower-presses, see-saws —
all summer, splitting in the garage.

'The Sawmill' was inspired by Seamus Heaney's 'The Forge'. Heaney's poem reminds me of when I was a child and my father would disappear out of daylight and into the shed each Saturday. My father came from a farming background, and the way he worked our tiny city garden and the tools in the shed had the same kind of heartbeat, an inner rhythm and ritual that I immediately recognised in 'The Forge'.

I admire how Heaney reveals much about the blacksmith without identifying him as such. There is a kind of vocation, a deep concentration and patience about the craftsman which I tried to emulate in 'The Sawmill'. I also recognised these qualities in my parents, who were both from rural Wexford.

For me, 'The Forge' is not about the completion of the labour, it is all about the craft – and that is also true of poetry. 'The Sawmill' concerns a blissfully happy moment in time, brought about by the carpenter going patiently about his work. 'The Forge' captures a way of life that is changing, as 'The Sawmill' captures passing childhood. I admire Heaney's tactile rendering of language and I imagine he laboured over each word until he had found exactly the right one. This is why Heaney and his work are particularly meaningful to me. It is this crafting of language, from my perspective and with my voice, that I want to bring to poetry.

Diglossing

Benjamin Webb

I

So. In days not long gone by
I was handed *Death of a Naturalist*
with *Dulce et Decorum Est*,
and I hated both, and scoffed at Poetry.

But after a decade or more of the hard border
in the bright water which ran through my heart
I fell fumbling fecklessly into your word-hoard,
down Sweeney's well, past Grendel's mother,
and out into the Underworld, the deepest part
which stank of heat and rotting flax and farts
from ranks of sludging frogs in stagnant waters.

I stumbled backward years beneath the Irish sea
with recognition ripping through like snare-fire
and confusion a half-heard hound-high choir
of demon voices — and now, my ears unplugged, I'm free
to listen, to blindly clamber higher
and be like Owens, below the wire,
doppelgänger mirror-walking to meet the enemy:

myself.

Self surfaced in the south of England,
enemy territory, where smirking arrogance spanned
years of being rulers of untold wealth
seeded by division — and which in Northern Ireland
I was somehow part of, being half-clanned
in Irish soil by an English father, without the stealth
to hide that if I 'pined', it was a different sound
to 'pound' —
      a silver-spooned shibboleth.

     II
So now abroad I grapple with these hasped lines,
these words I'd heard my uncles say,
now hammered into printed page.
          And the rhymes.
'Irish Rhymes' they call them, gently laid
down like garnets in gold-rimmed interlace,
delicately chiming.

       But their glint
is not too perfect — perfection
is not the way with us, too torn
by years of us and them, towns twinned
with accent-dappled names from shores
we'd never hope to visit, or
those fada-doubled names yet more distant,
          graffiti-painted acts

of resistance or of vandalism
or echoed cries from hate-soaked chrisms
of tar and tears which fill the tracks
scored out in ground a constant prison.
But amidst all the scars the pen starts digging
and rhymes fill up the cracks
         and heal.

Sweeney, perched in feathers at the edge of the dark
to rebuild the farmyard stuck burning, a cart
broken sends spinning that still self-slaughtering wheel
of us and us. But the rhymes gleam in the dirt.
They sparkle and ripple deeps-down in the murk
that brims in the well where you captured the sky.

When I was hardly born you stood
at a grave in Wessex, by the darkling thrush,
seeing that we all rhyme faintly in the lush
interlace of tongues and borderless fluidity
                                            of blood.

This poem concerns Heaney's place in my own psyche as a representation
of Irish identity. In school, somewhat bewildered by the strangeness of
poetry in general, Heaney was particularly off-putting for reasons that are
only now becoming clear. He represented the (Northern) Irishness that
I felt cut-off from as a town-dweller in a farming family, with a tinge of
an English accent, mocked when I started secondary school. My reaction
then was fuelled by anger at the sense of not belonging. I leaned into my
English identity, despite having few memories of ever living there. Later
Heaney began to appeal, but only through my interest in the poetry of Ted
Hughes, who represented almost an English version of the rural identity I
was apart from. It was only when I went to study in England that I began to
change. Now I was told my accent was Irish. There was often indifference,
at times arrogance, towards Northern Ireland and its history. The flaws of
home were no greater than the flaws of this new place. Reading Heaney's
Beowulf, especially his use of familiar Ulster dialect words to translate this
archetypally 'English' poem, brought Ireland closer just as I was becoming
distanced from England. Studying Irish led to further engagement with
poetry and with my own identity. It has been a strange journey, whereby
the work of a poet who once represented something I was not a part of is
now a reminder of home.

Dad's still in a coma so I'm sent

Jake Hawkey

beyond the hospital doors for five bags of chips,
three cod, plenty of salt and vinegar, mayonnaise
for my little sister. When I return, Dad's mother —
whose name I have always loved: Pamela
and whose mother's name I have loved more:
Elizabeth May West — says *Ark, put these chips
below his nose, see if he don't wake up then.*
Hahaha, applause in the family room.

When the others were away at football
I was all hers as we peeled potatoes
and Dad broke the silence falling through the door
with mud up his back and news of the final score.
Mum's chips with fried eggs when all was good.
Look at me, I've found the biggest chip in the world!

Seamus Heaney's sonnet sequence 'Clearances' is a marvel of construction. Operating simultaneously as 'private confession and public memorial' (qtd.)[1], the fabric of the language is both 'inside and outside the tribe' (qtd.)[2]. I considered these well-wrought sonnets while trying to understand the passing of my father. I wanted to create poems in his tongue, to be understood inside and outside our place. There were less potatoes in our house, but more chips; less God and more football. Having moved to Belfast a few years ago, I often feel distant from London, from my home, both physically and spiritually. Heaney's sonnets remind me of the universality in our need to be loved and understood by those we seek to love and understand; the inevitable pain in that, as well as the joy.

1   Ryan, Jennifer. 'The Transformative Poetics of Wanda Coleman's 'American Sonnets'', *African American Review* 48:4 (2015), pp 415–29.
2   Burt, Stephen. "The Contemporary Sonnet' in A D Cousins and Peter Howart (eds), *The Cambridge Companion to the Sonnet* (Cambridge, 2001), pp 245–66.

The Good Turf

Connie Roberts

Autumn, New York City, 1998, a silver-thatched man in a tweed jacket and collared shirt walks into a nondescript Irish bar. The hostess from Galway with the Bord Fáilte smile greets the man; he responds with a warm nod and hello before hoisting himself up on a stool at the long, black, lacquered counter. It is a Monday evening. Only a few after-work hair-of-the-dog stragglers. The baby-faced bartender from Roscommon serves the man a drink. Taking into account the man's garb and gait, the hostess surmises he's one of the many fathers over from Kerry or Cavan visiting the son or daughter in New York. The mother is down in Chinatown haggling over fake Louis Vuitton handbags or Gucci purses. She sidles up for the auld chat, about the exchange rate or the airfare.

"Oh, I hope the pound to dollar was lucrative for yeh, now."

"Sure, they'd rob-yeh-blind, Aer Lingus."

The man is up for the auld chat and gives as good as he gets. At one stage, he remarks on a Galwegian turn of phrase. The hostess thinks nothing of it till, an hour into the conversation, she finds out – and not from the man himself, mind you – she is in the company of a poet. A Nobel Laureate, no less. I don't believe it, Seamus Heaney! Now, the hostess who hasn't stumbled across a poem since her Leaving Cert *Soundings* anthology, had indeed heard on the telly a few years earlier that our Seamus had trotted over to Sweden for that illustrious award.

"Congratulations on winning the Peace Prize," she gushes, mixing up her Nobels.

Under his black, bushy eyebrows, Seamus' eyes crinkle into a smile.
Whatever you say, say nothing.
"Thank you," he nods humbly.

The hostess grabs an American Express reservation place card off a dining table and asks the Great Poet if he'd mind writing a note for her friend. She's Irish, you know. From Offaly. She's a waitress here, in this nondescript Irish bar in downtown Manhattan. She's off tonight, but, she'll be working Thursday night. Studying for her Bachelor's degree in English out on Long Island. Writes poems, so she does. She won $100 for one poem.

Seamus places the American Express reservation card on the black, lacquered counter and writes:

Connie,
It is a far, far better thing you do now than you have ever done. Stick with it.
S. Heaney

God, she'll be delighted with that now. Thanks a million. The hostess carefully places the note in an envelope for safe keeping.

The hostess with the Bord Fáilte smile, the baby-faced bartender and the Great Poet with the smiling eyes continue chinwagging. The suburban stragglers head for Grand Central and Penn. Someone puts quarters in the jukebox, and the singing begins.

"Give me back that note for your friend, the poet," Seamus quips.
He adds:

I believe you got a prize for poetic excellence. Congratulations.
Keep digging for the good turf.

Please excuse the writing.
PTO [Please turn over]

I want half of your $100. Hope to see you on Thurs.

The Great Poet doesn't make it back to the downtown nondescript Irish bar on Thursday evening. He pops in on the Wednesday to extend his apologies, via the bartender, to the poet-waitress. Something about having to fly to Canada a day earlier. Sure, they all want a piece of him now.

The poet-waitress is delighted with the note. Thanks a million. She loves Seamus Heaney. His surefootedness and sense of place. And ahh, Mossbawn and the green helmeted pump. A far cry from the pigeon-grey orphanage yard she grew up in.

The poet-waitress gets her degree. And another one. She hangs up the apron; takes down the spade. Starts digging for the good turf.

Don't forget your shovel if you want to go to work.

She wants to memorialise fellow industrial school survivor and activist Peter Tyrrell, who ended his own life in 1967 by immolating himself in a London park. She leans on Seamus Heaney. Peter Tyrrell deserves the very best, she thinks.

Seamus' iconic poem 'The Tollund Man' is about an Iron Age, naturally mummified body found in a bog in Denmark in 1950. Archaeologists believe that he was a human sacrifice, an offering to the gods, for a better harvest perhaps. In her poem 'Letterfrack Man', she views Peter Tyrrell's self-immolation as an act of sacrifice. After years of trying to inform the powers that be of abuses that occurred, and were occurring, in Irish industrial schools, in the ultimate form of protest, he offered himself up.

The executed leaders of the 1916 Easter Rising are hailed as martyrs, and rightly so. Peter Tyrrell, born in 1916, should also go down in the history books as a valiant warrior and heroic martyr.

The former waitress goes on to teach in the academy. She marries, has a son. Her son knows how much she loves Seamus Heaney. Didn't he have to suffer through recordings of his poetry, poetry, poetry on the week-long drive in the RV to Yellowstone, Big Sky Country? The 8-year-old-boy likes to taunt his mother with "Seamus Heaney wears a bikini!" before running off laughing.

Friday, August 30th, 2013, the poet-professor wakes up in a white clapboard house on a lawn-worship street in a New York suburb. She can't believe the headlines in the online Irish newspaper. The Great Poet can't be gone – wasn't she just on stage with him?

In haste, she emails Irish poet and mentor Brian Lynch, who had penned a tribute to Seamus in *The Independent*. Tells him that the Great Poet had visited her in a dream last night, the very night he lay in a hospital bed in Dublin.

She is at a poetry festival, quietly mouthing her poem 'Letterfrack Man' before going on stage, when she feels a presence over her left shoulder. She turns around to find Seamus Heaney smiling down at her. He isn't the frail Seamus of late, but the robust figure from 20 years earlier, with the shock of white hair and sideburns. With more than a bit of the divil in his eye, he suggests that they read 'The Tollund Man' and 'Letterfrack Man' in tandem.

He starts: "Some day I will go to Aarhus."

She follows: "One day I will go to Hampstead Heath
                to read his postscript, written in
                oily black ash that Friday in April.
                In that hollowed ground
                where they found him,
                his last meal, a pint & take-away,
                burnt offerings,
                his woollen overcoat melted to the bone…"

The dream ends with the Great Poet throwing his arms in the air with dramatic flair as he exits the stage. His final words to her:

"I'll leave you to it."

Bog Cotton

Sonya Gildea

Picking bog cotton on Árainn Mhór
we lie back to its peated edges
the Atlantic live about us
our voices rinsing in its charge

Driving then, across the north
to find the yearling plot
— unadorned still and to the side —
we unwrap three stems
of bog-made cotton

and leave them, for you
where they lay —
their stems to your feet
their white to your sky

The poem 'Bog Cotton' is written, in part, to Seamus Heaney and in closing becomes perhaps a small prayer of thanks. The day of the poem, almost a year after he died, was a warm day in July on an island off the west coast of Donegal before travelling on to Bellaghy.

There have been countless times in my life when I have been given something unexpected, necessary and sustaining in Seamus Heaney's work; in the way in which he pursued his practice; and perhaps, above all, in the love with which he sought to understand us, to know us and to celebrate us.

Walking the Same Cut

Kate Caoimhe Arthur

My mentor is the fine art printmaker, Iona Howard. I don't know that she knows she is my mentor. If asked, I suspect she would say that she is my friend, or, more generously, my collaborator. Both of these things are true; in fact, the lack of definition of the role that Iona plays in my life is something I find helpful.

I met Iona's work before I met her, though we live in the same village. I had not long moved here and was yet to experience the flat, agricultural land as anything other than cold and empty. Driving north towards Ely, on a road alarmingly right-angled with the crop of potato and leek coming almost right up to the car, I had a sense of being stranded. Underneath me, the road gulped and stuttered as if great, armour-plated, megalithic sea-creatures were rolling and flicking their bodies just below the surface. As it is built over the drained fen, the tarmac is laid on soil that is gradually eroding, causing it to crack and necessitate frequent re-surfacing. This makes travelling on it feel a bit like being on a rollercoaster, or as if the road is attempting to shake you off – I can never decide which. I accepted its hostility at face value.

When I saw Iona's enormous black-and-white carborundum prints of the fen, I started to suspect I was missing something. The big sky, so characteristic of the East Anglian landscape, was not the dominating feature. Instead, the texture of the black soil is lovingly rendered in the foreground, reaching up and away to the unnaturally even furrows of an intensively farmed field. Hay stubble can be picked out across its surface, with the thready detail of telegraph pole, hedgerow and outhouse on the horizon. It was breathtaking, intimate, beautiful. I began to fall in love.

On becoming the Fenland Poet Laureate in 2017, I knew I wanted to work with Iona and set about trying to persuade her. She understood that our meetings would have to fit around the feed times of my six-week-old. I discovered that she also had three children, now teenagers, and had plenty of experience negotiating the practice of her craft around the demands of family life. She accepted the inevitability of certain necessities, such as sickness or term dates, casting their net over my time and attention. She also encouraged me, where possible, to push back on these endless demands. The sense of validation that this recognition and encouragement brought me was liberating. We soon discovered that we drew inspiration from the same landscape. We had been walking the same Cut along the stretch of lode between our village and the next, and the long straight drove which bordered the north-east boundary of our village, apparently marking the very edge of the fen – she with her dog and me with my buggy, or, in the early mornings, alone.

So Iona agrees to be part of an artistic collaboration neither of us can describe yet. We are both excited by the idea of exploring the fens further. We talk about going deep into the heart of the fens. We start to make plans for finding and capturing some more essential, unseen part of the fen. In the meantime, we meet once or twice a week to follow our familiar route in the company of Meg, Iona's beautiful black standard poodle. As we walk, Iona draws my eye to the horizon. It's the detail of human endeavour she finds captivating: the water tower in the distance, Ely Cathedral even further. I have not especially noticed this before. I point out the pattern that the tractor has left ploughing the rich deep soil, the little kingdoms that are made when the soil is turned like that. It surprises me, considering how many of her pictures seem to be depicting the soil, that she is not as focused on it as I am. Iona knows her birds from sight and sound, and I begin to learn them from her. As spring takes firmer hold, the colours warm. Summer comes. We delight in each detail of this change. The swan cob and his mate, then the swan nest, then the downy cygnets. The distinction between the movement of a roe deer from a muntjac, at a distance. She helps me to see it, and also to name it.

She suggests lending me some of her work, and it comes to live in my house. I am scared of damaging it. I won't let the children into the room where I keep it. I try to write poems based on what I can see in her work, but I am not satisfied with them.

One of the attractions of working with someone who is not in your field is that it allows for a sense of companionship which is devoid of comparison. There is no rivalry or fear of influence. The standards we measure ourselves against are different, and we can complain about self-imposed or external limitations without fear, confident of sympathy. We are interested in one another's craft without knowing it from the inside.

A striking difference between the practice of printmaking and the practice of poetry is that in the former, you are building an image brick by brick to completion. An error, however tiny – even in the last moments of construction – can ruin the whole thing. This seems horrifying to me. I wouldn't know how to think if I couldn't bargain with the fact that anything can be erased, modified or hidden at a later point, with a critical eye. Another difference is the equipment required. Iona has a studio at home, with a printing press, where she can work late into the night with her door shut against the lure of family life. But she has become an expert at working, insofar as she can, *en plein air*. Taking sheets of acetate and a variety of drypoint needles for scoring, a tub of carborundum – like glistening files of earth – and a sketchbook, she can perch for several hours and work off the precise moment she is drawn to. We arrange times to do this together; me with a notebook and the Notes app on my phone, Meg dozing near us.

In search of the real fen, we visit Wicken Fen, which is a short drive away. It is one of a few tiny patches of ancient fenland still remaining, managed by the National Trust. With its whispering reeds and Konik ponies, it is beloved of walkers and birders. We often sit in a hide and work in companionable silence. I ask myself, does this feel more like a fen than the one I know? The one where the fields are bleached neon with glyphosate between plantings? 'What is the fen anyway?' I ask Iona. She does not quite know either.

When time allows, we plan trips further afield. A couple of times we visit a private nature reserve at Kingfishers Bridge. It seems a little eerie, perhaps just unfamiliar enough to make us feel out of place. We do not see a single other person, though there is a recently updated board with a tally of bird sightings. Walking the ridge which marks the perimeter of the land, we gain an excellent view of a large field covered with an enormous sheet of thin white plastic, to protect the early crops. The strong wind creates waves and ripples across the surface, revealing – at the edges – glimpses of the dark black fen soil. It is breathtaking; it is very like the sea. I feel suddenly homesick. Having grown up beside the sea I have never managed – living in England as I have done for about twenty years – to shake the claustrophobic feeling of being hemmed in by land. I want to stay right here by this synthetic sea, and I want to be at home by the real sea, in the same moment.

We decide to mount an exhibition with the work we have created. It's in a Cambridge gallery, where Iona is represented. As the time comes to hang the exhibition, Iona is full of questions that I have never considered: how do I want the poem to relate to the images visually and spatially? What paper do I want to print on? Do I want the work to float from the wall or hang? Have I noticed the aesthetic, three-dimensional effect that certain fonts and inks can create? I have never given these matters any thought – the space on my screen, from one line to the next, being the height of my interest in the matter. But once I have been guided through these considerations I cannot unsee them; I start to ask them of my own work.

Our explorations become more adventurous but, in certain other ways, less satisfying. We pick our way through a flooded landscape at Sutton Gault, finding it easy to imagine a time when the land would have looked like that for much of the year: sailing up to Ely in a skerry though malaria-infested water. We examine a Neolithic village, in which a wooden walkway has been preserved for thousands of years in the generous secret-holding peat. All of it is interesting and informative, but neither of us can find a way in.

'I only ever work from people and places that I know well,'[3] writes Celia Paul, describing her lifelong commitment to painting her mother and her sisters, luminous with love. We go back to working our local walks into our day, grateful for the return this year of the Great White Egret on the Cut. I tell Iona of my eagerness to buy a house here, having never bought a house anywhere. I feel that, then, the land will have to agree that it belongs to me and I to it; that I won't be a stranger.

The Irish have been coming to this part of the world for generations. Waterbeach, a nearby village, was a destination for waves of famine migrants. My own father used to come to work in the fields and canning factories here on his university vacations. I think about them as I plan to return to live in Northern Ireland. I wonder whether it felt like home to any of them, whether they stayed in the fens or returned to Ireland. Iona does not need the fen to love her. It exists, she exists; there are other places, she says. Meg bounds ahead of us; she remembers a moment a year ago when a rabbit was seen quivering in that exact spot.

3   Celia Paul, *Self-Portrait* (Jonathan Cape, 2019), p. 3.

Titanic

Roan Ellis-O'Neill

I have seen changes on the Newtownards
road: the 4*a* bus replaced by the *Glider*,
fish & chip shops beside burrito bars;
and rainbow flags flittering outside the pub.
Yet, the election posters never fall.
The *Glider* takes us faster into town,
but the old man is still figuring out
the ticket machine; no one to take his
change. I heard the gin-sipping woman say
'We never had burritos at your age!'
That was her proxy for change and progress.
Where did history disappear? I have
never taken the *Glider* past City Hall.
Peace travels along stranger roads.

A couple of years ago, the Glider replaced my beloved 4a bus. I hate everything the Glider stands for – the neoliberal façade of progress, speed, and free Wi-Fi. We can no longer see the city from the wondrous heights of the 4a double-decker; instead, its single-decker replacement delivers people as if they are parcels. Initially, I struggled to write through these concerns because they were melodramatic and, quite frankly, ridiculous.

When I read 'Epic' by Patrick Kavanagh for the first time, I realised that documenting seemingly insignificant events and objects – buses included – are neither ridiculous nor melodramatic. The more I studied his poems and essays, the more I revered how Kavanagh sought to develop a praxis that is both inclusive and individual: not solely concerned with audience and legacy, but more aligned with place and experience.

When I have been away from home for long periods, how I viewed the place I grew up in narrowed in scope; memories faded and connections dissipated. Kavanagh's approach revitalised my work in which I understood the value of staying 'local': not to adopt a parochial, monolithic attitude toward home, but to espouse a poetics that gives way to the phenomena of the everyday and how it is informed and animated by place. Kavanagh's ghost is very much present in 'Titanic' and the poems I wrote after. His presence, neither haunting nor authoritarian, emancipates dispossessed experiences and transforms them into moments of political, historical, and personal valence.

Cone

Emma Must

One landed in my yard today,
not pine nor fir nor spruce,
but traffic.

I am trying to see it
not as a threat,
but a gift.

It is heavier than a hoover.
It is quite battered.
It has three parts.

The base is a spongy square of black
with slightly bevelled edges,
rounded corners.

The body is red plastic,
the colour and shape
of a chilli pepper.

It has a shiny jacket
whose surface
prisms form

a pattern of octagons &
four-pronged stars
which fit

into one another
like a Moorish
mosaic.

O! I looked inside the vertex.
The centre of the base
is hollow:

not a slab,
but a
nut.

I'm fortunate to have had two great poetry mentors. Firstly, Mimi Khalvati, whose 'Versification' and 'Finding the Form' classes I sought out at the Poetry School in London, back in the days when creative writing courses in universities barely existed. You had to really scrabble around to find expert poets to teach you their craft when you couldn't make any further progress on your own. I was living on the Isle of Wight at the time and travelled to Mimi's classes by boat and train once a week, to learn the magic of what she had to teach. My second great mentor has been Sinéad Morrissey. The chance to learn from her, as well as Ciaran Carson and Leontia Flynn – three world-class poets whose work I'd been reading for years – was what inspired me to move to Belfast a decade ago.

Mimi taught me the nuts and bolts of form, which unlocked poetry for me. Sinéad added to this groundwork with her rigorous feedback ('Cut!') and especially her war on 'scaffolding': those bits of wooden language that can be axed from a poem to make its lines more sleek, without it falling over. She also deepened my love of syntax – the mechanical energy with which a poem flows. So: thank you, Mimi; thank you, Sinéad, for helping my self-seeded joy in writing poetry to grow and stand up on its own.

A Sweathouse at Killavallig

Kevin Cahill

Instead of burying him, I stand Tomás O'Leighin
up on his feet, letting him gather his breath
there by the fire, the hardwood dowels
hammered into his joints, keeping him steady.

Our Bronze Age ancestors held people together
in the house for as long as possible: familiar spirits
dangling in a corner,
or friends you could talk to in the middle of the night, or people
you could still learn something from. So that day,
seven hundred years ago, Tomás, the famous bonesetter
from Blarney, got pushed around by weather
blowing in from the East...
feeling the roof and low door of the country
turn into something like a sweathouse —
four by seven feet long, near a pool of water
five feet deep.

With our eyes to the ground
each new wave rearranges
the flowers in our garden...our fingers
drum on the cocktail of our blossoms
in time with the battles. It turns out
flowers they call in the West Country
Oliver-Cromwell's-Creeping-Companions
are natives showing up in our own lands.

This poem is inspired by former Ireland Professor of Poetry, Michael Longley. His work uses the phonetic and folkloric layers of Ireland's flora to convey meaning in subtle and powerful ways. Throughout his work, wild thyme, sphagnum moss, brambles, fuchsias, twayblades and heathers deepen our sense of things – from romance to violence, from loss to the endless plenitude of our world. I am working on a book of poems which gathers its semantic momentum from incorporating the historical and ecological energy of the Irish floral landscape, or, more specifically, the common floral landscape of the British Isles as a whole. The flowers I select in each poem contribute a sense of unity, crossing thresholds and borders, giving glimpses of natural freedoms of movement. Michael Longley was innovative enough to make a poem exclusively from the names of flowers. For me, this is a good template to approach and conceive my own work.

What Became of the Horses

Orla Fay

after Michael Longley's 'The Horses'

Imagining the fall of Patroclus,
and with the spent rage of Achilles
still haunted by those ashen features,

I walk past the faded stables
in deep green fields, by sleeping castles,
the main gates stripped of paint.

The animals kept were promises, dreams
defeated in battles by hardships and losses,
beaten down, their spirits depleted.

Above the red-brick pillars of the entrance
to history the leaves of a copper beech stir.
Xanthos and Balios are awakened by their father

the West Wind, their distant hoofbeats disturb
the ants, making the wild rose tremble,
this softest rustling, enough to soothe a jaded heart.

I like to think they gallop through eternity,
that they can be summoned by those in need,
their tears stellar ointment to the wounded.

I first read 'The Horses' around 2002 or 2003 in the Bloodaxe Books anthology, *Staying Alive*. I was moved by the image of the loyal horses in mourning for slain Patroclus. Their 'hot tears' evoked the depth of the upset and I admired their nobility, their steadfastness in the face of 'threats and sweet-talk and the whistling whip'. Yes, I thought, these were traits to aspire to. In this anthology, I also loved Longley's 'At Poll Salach Easter Sunday 1998'. I was stunned by its simplicity and beauty, and felt the excitement of 'A single spring gentian shivering at our feet.' The contrast in colour between the snow of the hills and the violet of the gentian is striking.

I enjoy finding threads to follow in Longley's work, and often look for ways to weave them into my own writing. I greatly admire his commitment to themes of peace and reconciliation, the promise of the future, and of ideals deserving fidelity. I remember 'Ceasefire' being an influential work during secondary school, when the peace process in Northern Ireland was being negotiated in the mid-1990s. This powerful poem employs Homer's *Iliad* to describe how men can swallow their pride and make sacrifices for peace. In my poetry, I, too, search for optimism and the goodness of the spirit. Longley's work has made me more courageous and faithful as a poet.

Ecce Homo

Helen Dempsey

The men who wear black serge, who don a cross with strokes
metamorphose from their loves, their lives and change
the dairyman to Mr. Hyde, the baker to Sweeney Todd,
the fireman - Jack the Ripper, the window-dresser - Captain Blythe.

They prowl, pounce on minor slights; gnawed raw potato skin,
weak salute, broken spade, late to rise, too slow to run, too weak to dig.

In bare bulb light the cellar door compounds his shadowed fright,
three burly men will curve him on a barrel's boards, drop his trousers to the floor,
flex a rubber hose. They will succeed

to fell a man
to hell a man
to starve a man
to carve a man
to dull a man
to cull a man
to turn a man
to spurn a man
to rag a man
to snag a man
to freak a man

to break a man
to sink a man
to brink a man
to tease a man
to freeze a man
to drill a man
to will a man
to dread a man
to head a man
to craze a man
to daze a man
to flay a man
to grey a man
to salt a man in every welt.

Their message to the listening horde: the *Übermensch* is best.
Pain-staggered soul drags his husk across the square to sick bay,
on the way they aim. Click. Whizz. Thud. Laugh. Inmates strip him bare.
In a pit they pile him meshed in limbs; quick-lime will claim his stare.

British Merchant Navy seaman and POW, Harry Callan from Derry, aged 20 years in 1944,
recorded this atrocity which took place in the Nazi Labour Education Camp, Bremen-Farge,
Lower Saxony, Germany.

Máighréad Medbh has mentored a poetry masterclass in Rathbeale Library, Swords, Co. Dublin, once a month, for several years and I have been privileged to attend it. She provides us with exercises to write innovatively.

This poem resulted from an exercise called 'The Body in the Poem/ Composing a poem based around an activity'. We worked on controlling the pace with line and word length to create sense impressions. In her latest book, *Parvit of Agelast: A Fantasy in Verse*, her poem 'Hide' mirrors the theme of the horrors of the camps during the Second World War.

I had the honour of preparing for publication *Forgotten Hero of Bunker Valentin: The Harry Callan Story,* by Michèle Callan. The regular punishment was twenty-five lashes of the rubber hose. In the course of researching the Bremen-Farge war trials for the book, I was struck by the innocuous occupations of the accused, recorded in their depositions, before they became Gestapo guards. With reference to Máighréad's exercise, I used twenty-five short mantra-like lines and the hard words, 'a man' to imitate the lashes of the hose.

Many years ago, I attended one of Máighréad's workshops. We stood, feet firmly on the ground, until she made us aware that our whole bodies were connected to the earth and to the heavens by a chord running through us expressed in poetry. Máighréad demonstrates this in her performances. Who is left to tell of the horrors of that war? I am tugging the chord.

Paula Meehan: Remembering Dublin

Kelly O'Brien

Much of Paula Meehan's poetry returns to her childhood in the North Dublin inner-city tenements on Seán McDermott Street, from which she was later relocated to Finglas in 1968 following their destruction and the subsequent displacement of that community. The clearance of the tenement buildings for development in the Dublin city centre was largely framed by the Irish State as progressive; the movement of the inner-city communities to the outer suburbs was viewed positively as the elimination of poverty. This understanding is what Michael Pierse describes as the 'widespread contemporary assumptions that the republic has become a more meritocratic, classless society.'[4] Yet as Pierse notes, the break-up of the inner-city community along with the construction of flats and council housing estates and the decline in traditional working opportunities led to the alienation of the Dublin working class and a rigidity of class structures within the republic.[5] Meehan's poetry is largely focused on the ways in which the Irish State frames progressive narratives about our history and our present, and the ways in which these narratives silence those who have been marginalised and neglected by that same state.

It is through memory that Meehan works to unearth a Dublin that is reflective of the city in which we live. Meehan has said in an interview: 'Is there such thing as a past? Or is there only a relationship with that past?

---

4   Michael Pierse, *Writing Ireland's Working Class* (Palgrave Macmillan, 2011), p. 21.
5   Pierse, *Writing Ireland's Working Class*, p. 21.

Poetry can be a tool for excavation. Do you dig? Remembering for its own sake wouldn't interest me, but memory as agent for changing the present appeals to me greatly. But you go back before you go forward.'[6] Memory then functions as an ethical undertaking for Meehan and a way in which to examine how we exist in the present.

Meehan is primarily concerned with how we commemorate and remember and *what* we commemorate and remember, both as individuals and as a collective nation and she has often used personal memories, predominantly from her childhood, to counteract a dominant state historical narrative that claims to be moving forward into a modern, European nation. Meehan writes from her position as a working-class woman, often focusing on a sense of urban dispossession and on the negligence of the Irish State as a way of interrogating how power structures within Irish society dictate the voices that are heard, the history that is constructed and thus the collective identity that is formed. Meehan works to complicate the linear history engendered by Irish Government through state commemoration by setting up an alternative Irish past within her poems that highlights voices she understands to have been neglected or silenced by the Irish State.

These concerns are integral to all of Meehan's work and are equally central to Meehan's most recent collection, *Geomantic*. In 2013, Meehan took up the three-year role of Ireland's Professor of Poetry and subsequently published the lectures she delivered during her time in the post. Both *Geomantic* and the published lectures titled *Imaginary Bonnets with Real Bees in Them* were published in 2016, the centenary of the 1916 Easter Rising. *Geomantic* is a more formal collection than any published by Meehan previously. As *The Irish Times* notes, *Geomantic* is comprised of almost a decade's worth of poems yet it is highly cohesive with the number nine playing a primary role; the collection consists of 81 poems of nine lines each and each line is nine syllables long. Meehan has said that the formal patterning of the collection was inspired by the quilts

---

6   Eileen O'Halloran, Kelli Maloy and Paula Meehan, "An Interview with Paula Meehan", *Contemporary Literature* 43, no. 1 (2002), p. 13.

made by families affected by drug use and the AIDS crisis in Dublin that were hung up at memorial services. She says: 'I felt, in this year of commemoration, 2016, that these quilts would be my inspiration and source, because they mean more to me, and speak more profoundly to me, than many of the 'official' or state commemorative gestures. If measured by the aspirations of the founding principles of the Republic, these communities have been betrayed.'[7] The neglect of vulnerable young people at the hands of the Irish State has long been a concern for Meehan, going back to poems in *Dharmakaya* such as 'The Lost Children of the Inner City' and further back to possibly Meehan's most famous poem 'The Statue of the Virgin at Granard Speaks'. With her use of the memorial quilts as inspiration, Meehan sets herself against the official memory of the 1916 commemorations in favour of remembering those who she believes have been excluded from the public narrative.

As such, the poems of *Geomantic* can be read as counter-commemorative, refusing the glorification of the Easter Rising and the Irish Nation. Specifically, in the second half of *Geomantic*, Meehan works firmly against the official memory in a sequence of poems that directly address the commemorations of the centenary of the 1916 Easter Rising. Meehan refuses the romanticism of the past perpetuated by the Irish Government and the clear-cut narrative that Emilie Pine has outlined as the emergence of the state out of trauma 'and into stability and modernity.'[8] However in the aftermaths of the Celtic Tiger, the bailout and the subsequent austerity, Meehan sees only ironies and falsities in the commemorative efforts of the Irish Government.

In *Geomantic*'s 'The Child I Was', Meehan remembers the 1966 commemoration of the Easter Rising and her blind belief in the romanticism of that event that had been taught to her: 'Nineteen sixty-six, eleven years / old, let me die for Ireland I prayed.'[9] Mary McAuliffe has written about

7   Paula Meehan, email to Kathryn Kirkpatrick, in "Memory in Paula Meehan's *Geomantic*", *Irish University Review* 47, No. 1 (2017): 12.

8   Emilie Pine, "*The Politics of Irish Memory*" (Palgrave Macmillan, 2011), p. 15.

9   Paula Meehan, *Geomantic* (Dedalus Press, 2016), p. 57.

the 2016 project at Richmond Barracks that aimed to recover the lost histories of the women who participated in the 1916 Rising. McAuliffe writes of the prominence of working-class women within the group: 'All of these women were from working-class backgrounds, many of them living in the tenements.'[10] However the lives of these women, who would have come from a similar place and background to Meehan, would have largely remained unknown to her. It is notable that female figures from upper-class backgrounds, such as Countess Markievicz, remained central to the history of the Rising. McAuliffe goes on to write that 'women's involvement in the Rising has been largely excluded from earlier commemorations. In particular, during the 50th anniversary of the Rising in 1966 the contribution of women was rarely mentioned.'[11] As such, the 1966 anniversary Meehan would have experienced as a schoolchild was presented as a history that largely excluded women, and particularly working-class women. Yet within the poem Meehan also illustrates the beginnings of sparks of imagination as she writes: 'I thought the O'Connell Monument / was all about the winged women / at its base.'[12] In this memory, Meehan exhibits an early impulse towards an alternative history, one which might place women at the forefront of the narrative. The first six lines of the poem largely trace Meehan's childlike inability to fully understand the complexity of the history of Ireland that has been taught to her both in school and by the monuments on the streets of Dublin. However in the final lines of the poem there is absolute clarity as Meehan articulates her understanding, even as a child, of the reality of her life and how it connected to public history, expressing the irony of her upbringing: 'I understood we were poor – we lived / on streets named for the patriot dead.'[13] These lines foreground the failure of the Irish State to uphold the values for which the leaders of the 1916 Rising died, and also the paradox

---

10 Mary McAuliffe, Liz Gillis, Éadaoin Ní Chléirigh and Marja Almqvist, "Forgetting and Remembering – Uncovering Women's Histories at Richmond Barracks: A Public History Project", *Studies in Arts and Humanities* 2, No. 1 (2016), p. 23.

11 McAuliffe, "Uncovering Women's Histories at Richmond Barracks", p. 27.

12 Meehan, *Geomantic*, p. 57.

13 Meehan, *Geomantic*, p. 57.

in renaming inner-city streets after those who died for Irish freedom only to allow the development of slums on those same streets. 'The Child I Was' unfolds in a typically Meehan format that pushes images of public monuments of historical memory such as the O'Connell Monument and Nelson's Pillar up against her own personal memories to expose the incongruency between the two.

'The Commemorations Take Our Minds Off the Now' sees Meehan at her most explicit as she outwardly criticises the Irish Government's use of the commemorations as a distraction from the state's failure to prioritise the needs of its citizens:

> A boon to the Government; they rule
> in the knowledge that none can keep track
> of just how much the country has
> been flogged like an old nag to within
> an inch of its life.[14]

Meehan accuses the Irish Government of unethically constructing memory; and the use of this memory as a method of creating an engineered and false narrative about post-crash Ireland and the effect austerity has had on the poor in Irish society: 'I commemorate / the poor going round and round the bend.'[15] Meehan presents here a counter-commemoration, focusing, as her poetry often does, on those forgotten within the construct of Irish history, bringing forward forgotten memories from her childhood in the newly established republic in order to examine the problems faced by Irish citizens in the present.

Throughout her life Meehan has worked tirelessly to highlight voices and communities that have been marginalised in Irish society: from family members dispossessed of their homes in the tenements and dislocated to the Dublin suburbs to communities devasted by drug use and the AIDS crisis. However, it is the highlighting of these lives through Meehan's own voice,

14   Paula Meehan, *Geomantic* (Dedalus Press, 2016).
15   Meehan, *Geomantic*, p. 58.

that of a working-class Dublin woman, that is what remains so remarkable about Meehan's work; hers is a voice rarely heard in Irish society, and even more rarely in Irish poetry. It is a voice that is both critical and warm, often funny and affectionate. In a time when the Irish State claims prosperity and Dublin city is increasingly geared towards tourism and large investors, and when the housing crisis makes the city inhospitable to its own citizens, it is the people of the city that inform Meehan's Dublin. In *Dharmakaya*, Meehan writes: 'My grandmother's hands come back to soothe me. / They smell of rain. They smell of the city.'[16]

16   Paula Meehan, ' Grandmother, Gesture', *Dharmakaya,* (Carcanet, 2000), p. 29.

A Book for This

Emily Holt

One Friday in the summer of 2020, we left the city and drove east to Kachess Lake in the Okanogan-Wenatchee National Forest. At camp that evening, as fighter jets scored the sky, one of the couples we were with asked us if the police response to local protests had escalated. That morning the president had threatened to send in federal forces to break up an occupied protest and arrest activists demanding that the city defund the police and invest in Black communities. My husband, who grew up in Washington, looked at the sky and replied calmly, *No, the Navy always practices here*. Still hearing the jets heading east, I looked at the contrails and thought of a poem by Paula Meehan, written, I would guess, around the time she was working on an MFA in Creative Writing at Eastern Washington University. In 'Chapman Lake: Still Life with Bomber,' from her 1985 collection, *Reading the Sky*, as a B52 bomber roars over a lake some 220 miles east, near the town of Spokane, Meehan observes, 'It is as much a part of this lake / As those pines, those flies.'

I think of this line whenever I am at risk of forgetting the extent to which the human and the wild not only intersect, but are irrevocably intertwined. Whenever I am at risk of committing that white American sin of looking at the forests, mountains, and waters of a region and not seeing that those lands were made wild in the way we now conceive of it through the displacement and genocide of Indigenous peoples. Along the Columbia Plateau, the lands of the Yakama peoples were methodically incorporated into national forests and wilderness areas – preserved from further settlement and resource extraction in the name of the most infamous of settler-colonial states, the United States of America.

Throughout the past few months of protest and pandemic, in particular, I have thought often of the final stanza of Meehan's poem: 'Pines, bomber, flies, lake, / Spread circles to ripple this America / I am reluctant heir to.' Having grown up in the coastal lands of northern California, I am in some ways more heir to this America than Meehan. Though my father grew up in Ireland, in the same town my maternal great-grandmother left after losing both of her parents in the 1918 pandemic, I am, by incident of my birth, American, and by incident of citizenship laws, also Irish. Yet Meehan's poem reminds us that we are not only responsible for or implicated in the lands where we were born or which legally claim us, but also those that we occupy and visit, those through which flow the water and air and nutrients on which we depend. In the past few weeks, in particular, as migrant workers strike in protest against dangerous conditions at fruit-harvesting operations across the state, conditions made only more dangerous by the current pandemic, I think of the fact that while studying for her MFA, Meehan also worked as a fruit harvester along the Columbia basin.

That the work of a poet – her creative practice, her texts, and the material ways in which she supported her writing – can enter the mind and body of another in this manner is proof of the extent to which mentors can shape the way apprentices like myself see poetry. As a first-generation student, I entered college wanting to be a journalist; it seemed the only profession in which writing could be compensated. Yet a single class with Samuel Green, the inaugural poet laureate of Washington state, fundamentally changed my conception of the duties and the position of the poet. Green, who lives in a self-built log cabin where he and his wife, Sally, print and hand-bind books of poetry, often writes of the rhythms of stewarding the land around him, the forests and meadows of a remote island off the Washington coast. He introduced me not only to Meehan and her work, but to the idea of the working poet. Poetry as I once saw it was the privilege of the few; in many ways, it still is, yet in the past thirty years, poets such as Green and Meehan have demonstrated, through their work, their generosity as teachers, and their daily lives, what it means to commit one's life to poetry. They have done so not by relying on the privileges of patronage, but rather by turning to the wells of poetic tradition, ancestral wisdom, and the truths learned by daily attunement with the earth.

I met Meehan once, years ago. It was a January of snow and burst pipes. I had graduated from college less than a year before. Rather than accepting an offer to study poetry at Queen's University, I had decided to take a position as a caregiver in Belfast. When I met Meehan, I was on my way back to California. What led me to abandon the position earlier than expected is still often opaque to me, though perhaps it shouldn't be. I have at times written that I left Belfast and returned to California in the midst of what others might call a breakdown. Still, I rarely use that term to describe a period when I did little more than run at night, read Kierkegaard, and spend a decent share of each day at the foot of my bed thinking of a long line of blue painkillers. I rarely use that term perhaps because on the January afternoon that my friend and I spent visiting with Meehan and her partner, poet Theo Dorgan, terms like *breakdown* or *depression* felt paltry in comparison with the breadth of human commitment and creativity we witnessed that day. As we walked along the beach, my friend talking with Theo about the theories of Maurice Merleau-Ponty, Paula and I watched her dog trot lightly in the sand. On the way back from the beach, we crammed into the backseat of the car and talked about our shared love of Van Morrison. At their house, I remember marvelling at the shelves and shelves of books. I remember a half-completed puzzle laid out on a low coffee table – the image was of a man in a garden, a towel draped over his head, a child bathing in a kiddie pool, the garden a lush chaos of flowers. I remember sipping whiskey in their kitchen, and Theo teasing us for being so quiet, and my friend quipping that he was from a long line of Montana ranchers. I remember the slightly dissociating thrill of a conversation that whirred between politics, poetry, philosophy, and climate change at a speed somewhere between that of my Irish family's dinner-table conversations and college seminars on Ancient Greece. As we were saying goodbye, Paula noticed that we weren't dressed warm enough and insisted that we at least take a pair of her gloves. I remember standing on the train platform in that soft yellow sodium light, looking at my hands thinking, *I am wearing Paula Meehan's gloves.*

In the years since, my belief in the place of writing – as agent of change, as mirror, as balm – has been tested. When my mother was dying a few summers ago, she turned to me and asked, *Is there a book for this?* She didn't need an antecedent. I knew how much we both wanted the page to provide what doctors and priests and even hospice could not. At the time, I was reading *Imaginary Bonnets with Real Bees in Them*, a text I read to her in snippets between sleep. Because of the nature of grief, the text's effect on me that hot and too-brief summer seemed to fade once the funeral was over, when fall came and I returned to the false fever of a university schedule. But it remained, in a deep, physical sense. A year later, at a reading in Dublin, while reading a poem about losing her mother, Meehan nearly lost her voice and breath halfway through, and I lost the nerve to walk up and reintroduce myself. Instead I slipped out to Bewley's and ordered tea and read poems until the shaking stopped. It takes a certain courage not simply to write loss, but to speak it into a room.

I have written academically about Meehan's influence, and the formal brilliance of her work – from poetry to essays to plays. But I am writing these reminiscences now to make a point about the complexity of the idea of mentorship. Over the years, I have become increasingly hesitant to claim any poet as a mentor, especially as I begin to teach writing myself. In part because too strong of an association often brings with it an even stronger need to break free, to create a voice and breath and texture that is one's own. And even more because it seems to stake a claim in the fields of a mentor's talent, as well as staking a claim in their private life. The more that we see poets as extraordinary minds and spirits living in the ordinary, shared spaces of city buses and waiting rooms and grocery aisles, the more poetry seems both possible for more of us, and beautifully ordinary. The more we might find it written in the 'Northside graffiti of a morning,' lit by the 'acid colours along the train line,' and peopled by the 'elders and the unemployed dreaming, / radiant in the winter sunshine…'[17]

17   Paula Meehan, 'The Beauty (Of It)', *Geomantic* (Dedalus Press, 2016), p. 67.

The musician of the lake

Art Ó Súilleabháin

Dad stumbled through tunes on the box,
sounded windy on the long ebony flute,
blew foul notes through the saxophone,

stuttered on a Clarke's penny whistle,
but when he took a split cane fly rod,
a fibre glass, a carbon mix, a graphite

or a composite, he made it sing perfect
notes, tunes of casting. A silk line flew
through the eyes, curled in the wind,

unfurled eight metres out, landed quietly,
sank intact into waves, coloured feathers
tempted the scales below. Drew the line

back smoothly or in varied movements,
through gnarled fingers, judging length,
played the nylon in further enticement,

lifted the rod slowly to ten o'clock, then
snapped into a graceful curve behind him,
engaged in yet another perfect symphony.

Bone Road by Geraldine Mills played a significant role in the creation of this work. Her writing takes the ordinary history of her family and makes a collection of poems from it. Both the work and Geraldine herself have inspired me to take the minutiae of my own family history and to create from it. Her poem 'He Longs for Bog Cotton' generated a memory for me and the word 'flick' in the last line reminded me of how my father Michael John 'flicked' his split-cane fishing rod in such a way as to make the line spool out over the wave and yet land smoothly. He too spent some time in America but longed for his home in north Galway and the Corrib, the lake of his childhood. He came back there in the 1960s, with his wife Alice and two children, just like the ancestors of Geraldine Mills returned to Mayo despite the poverty that it offered. Her celebration of this going and returning in *Bone Road* created in me the need to honour memories that ran deep in my own psyche.

Beyond the Meadow

Jackie Gorman

They spin in the current
near the open lock-gate.
I am mesmerised by these otters,
these whirling water dervishes.

Sharp bone-crushing teeth
bite down on what they want.
They gnaw through to the marrow.
I envy their instinct, their knowing.

Their tails slap the water
with a heavy thump.
Maybe this is what
happiness sounds like.

I think when I die
this is where I will go,
to these otters.

They will be waiting
to show me life
underwater –
loud, dark and
sometimes frothy.

I will be carried away
by a raft of otters
to their holt, beyond
the meadow,
the scent of summer.

My work has been strongly influenced by early mentoring I received from Noel Monahan. A thoughtful poet and a generous teacher, Noel's own work is often concerned with seeing the magic and mythic in what others may perceive as ordinary. He has an uncanny ability to encourage new poets to trust their own perception of the world. He is also not afraid to encourage a poet to go a little further when necessary. His early advice still comes to me. I was writing a lot about nature but there was no undertow: animals and birds were just that, not the harbingers and messengers I have come to see them as now. He said to me 'you can't be looking into the same ditch the whole time'. He's right, you have to find different places and perceptions for poetry. He's also concerned with place and how poetry can map a landscape; the midlands is not as well mapped in poetry as other parts of Ireland. In his own work, Noel is a cartographer with words and an encouraging guide for so many writers in the region. His poem 'Advice to a Young Poet,' recently published in *The Irish Times*, probably sums it up:

. . . .

Stay in the field with its mysteries
Sift through the grass with the brown hare
Listen to the hills clapping hands,
Crab apples dropping into the ditch.
If you remain long enough
You'll feel the warmth of a candle burning inside you,
The blur of its flame constantly changing.

After Your Reading

Tim Dwyer

May 2016

Life at a slant,
wound as a gift,

standing at the podium,
your voice grows strong —

With all my circling
a failure to return.

After the reading, I shake your hand,
imagine I am your student
forty years ago.
You give me a book from your shelf,
a poet you say might suit me well.

We talk about Brooklyn stoops
from different eras —
your uncle, the fiddler,
runs a speakeasy downstairs;
my father tends bar on the corner,
pours shots for men far from home.

With all their circling,
they never return.

Stillness in a stream,
you hold the speckled trout
in your cupped hands —
as in your poetry,

never in the way
of legendary obstacles.

Opening lines based on Theo Dorgan's introduction of, and conversations with, John Montague at the American Irish Historical Society in New York. Other lines taken from and inspired by John Montague, Collected Poems: 'Rough Field: Home Again,' 'The Locket,' 'The Country Fiddler,' 'The Trout,' and 'All Legendary Obstacles.'

Younger writers need older ones to look up to
— John Montague, Second Childhood

In my university days, I was a poetry student in a creative writing program. One of my professors, Stuart Friebert, was an excellent teacher who encouraged me to pursue the craft. Following university, my personal and professional decisions took me away from writing for 30 years.

When I began writing again ten years ago, I became very engaged with current Irish poetry, and Irish journals were receptive to my work. I was especially drawn to the voice and sensibility of John Montague's poetry.

I met John at the New York *PoetryFest* in 2012. Although I was in my mid-fifties and our friendly conversations were brief, I gently envied those who had been his students. When I met him again four years later, at his last reading in New York, I wished he had been one of my mentors. On the train home that evening, I wrote the first draft of this poem and through the writing, my wish came true.

Like meadows under flood, the young people.

Jerm Curtin

Like meadows under flood, the young people.

At school one day, James, a boy
representing one clan in a local feud,
was ambushed by a posse from the enemy,
and outnumbered, five to one.
I stood with Lynch and watched
as the unfortunate got pricked
and goaded with various sharp objects.

Lynch and I were marched through
every class for punishment.
We had failed to halt the brutality.
Lynch was to die in his teens, victim
of a hit and run, the driver unidentified.
You'd wonder what the Joes you meet
might carry on their consciences.

Later, in Cork, a junkie I knew as Bob
mentioned someone from my quarter
he'd encountered in the mental home.
It turned out to be James,
admitted for wearing his mother's clothes
about the house. After what I'd seen him suffer
for his family, it didn't seem the worst of crimes.

Bob had been addled by addiction,
but had come round in a pool of guilt.
A ritual he'd held to conjure up supply —
the details of which he did not tell —
condemned him to the dregs of an existence,
disowned by family, friends dead,
his girl cold as a stone at his side.

I had given him no thought in years.
I had buried the past like a litter
of pups. But when I heard the poet
was gone and took his books
so long unread down from the shelves,
a dam burst like a river that finds
its native course when engineering fails.

The Wild Rose, Like Dolmens ...
granite blocks exposed, or the words
of an old neighbour on the bohereen.
He hit our sour culture clean on the head,
and I had run from what I saw.
Now I know we cannot think or feel
without the tools of metaphor and form.

I cross a field where bog was drained,
grass shivering where ferns once climbed
the Iron Age mound and trench
of a fulach fia. Hedgerows and dry walls,
empty cottages and ancient sites flattened,
torn up, the stones removed, only old potato
drills cross-hatching the silent meadows.

Formless, they drown in winter rains.

In Cork in the eighties, when poetry was still for me an undercover, embarrassing activity – fine enough in faraway places like New York or Northern Ireland – John Montague was a beacon. He looked like a poet, stylish and cosmopolitan, but he also straddled the divide between the rural Ireland I was longing to escape and a glamorous outside world I could only aspire to. I read his books, then packed them away somewhere at the back of my mind before finally leaving Ireland.

I hardly knew him, but, when he died in 2016, I was saddened. I took the books down and began to reread poems I hadn't seen in a very long time. It was a moment of inspiration, the beginning of one of my most extraordinary experiences as a reader, re-encountering what I now realised were my own roots as a poet. I knew all the poems so deeply, so intimately. I had read them at an age when I was completely open to influence, to the lure of a great writer's music. Montague was my master, and I was now seeing the source of so much of what I considered to be myself.

An Irish Emigrant Foresees a Day in NYC

Stephen de Búrca

after Paul Muldoon

Awesome, this May day and the tumult in the crowds
here at Grand Central Station.
Upon alighting, I'm happy to sit and avoid the cheerless clouds
and watch the people being rationed
into queues and groups like huge, splintering
families. The prelude to the station's tannoy
is not unlike a cuckoo ringing in spring
in Carna where my mother (who, hoy-hoy,

shares Christian names with the woman
who introduced GH Lees to Dubbleya-Bee)
lived in sin with a son in her womb,
the first of two by a man known affectionately
as T to avoid
the anglicised pronunciation of Tomás.
I get up to leave (the tannoy
giving my head a terrific ache) and outside the awesome

crowds are still tumultuous.
Blueshirts brownshirts turn-the-beat-around-shirts
there's no stopping the *nullius*
filius-ness of being in a place you've never before parsed.
Her father's parents (Michael and fair May-

god-be-with-you) were married here and had three of twelve
before returning (and-also-with-you) to Castledaly
but not before aul' Michael served

as a WWI medical orderly here in the US of A.
The pension and citizenship was enough to set up shop and farm
in Castledaly's Isle-a-Willa
half a mile down the road from
the village church,
as the owl flies, where Michael's brother (né Peter)
was accused with another man of ambushing a dúchrónach.
It was not the first time US Passports (né papers)

were put to legal use. I hear
Trump Tower isn't far, but for the craic,
part of me wants to Kiltartan-criss-and-Tullycross the East River
to Roosevelt Island Racquet
Club (doubtful there'd be mini-golf), though I'm craving a lonely impulse
of shellfish; I may fare well with one, not even hurl
or be repulsed
or even whiff at an oyster.

According to Google Maps, there's Dock's Oyster Bar
and Crave Fishbar and Grand Central
Oyster Bar (beneath me) and Oceana, all nearby,
but I am in a state of forgetful-
ness, *amnestia* even. T's mother, Pearl (née Esther) Cooke,
had never been to the States
I don't think, before her mini-strokes,
before she bought the house in Naas with sockets

so many she took pride in them,
after she married Tom (a tailor)
when she was sixteen or seventeen in Roscommon
when he was ten years her elder,

a man so good with his hands
it left him legless – a dubble-amputee
from diabetes (né fond-
of-the-drink-ism). I pass a Double Tree

Hilton, but he cut suits on Saville Row
not far from Hyde Park (Mayfair, not Roscommon) where I worked
in a café and learned to make cappuccinos
and lattes with my hands while I puckered,
tremendously hungover, hearing 'NYC Beat' for the first time. I don't know the truth-
nor-full-consequence of Tom's handiwork and homegrown
wood, but he built a caravan from scratch
which they took to Enniscrone

this side of Drumcliff and north of Mayo-god-help-us. T, only a gasúr
in those early days, had an awful
knack for wasting breath through unanswered
wails and howls and tantrums to much díomá,
howling so much it'd give life to the dead
only for it to be taken away. And now, there's Saint Thomas'
Church across from St Pat's and there are some squareheaded
blueshirted police officers

with thumbs under toolbelts
and shiny aviators taking nothing in,
not even a scratch. Before she could go for seconds, nothing could be left on
my mother's-mother's (Mary-wife-of-G) plate. The radio called in
the updates as her father, Trev, marked the map of Europe
on their dining room wall, upon which he pegged
it up to track the Axis' progress, whistling a chirrup.
A Blueshirt, no doubt, which cost him an arm and a leg

in terms of the Drumcolliher dispensary
he felt may have been, to be frank,
unfairly taken from him. He felt it necessary

to name Mary's youngest sister Franco
(not Frank O', god help us)
and the two of them disappeared piecemeal
into the woodwork (*nullius*
pavet occursum) at the end of each meal.

Trev's own brother, Arthur,
over Picardy's poppy fields, in an RAF Fairey IIIC,
was shot down during November's
amnesty at the age of nineteen or twenty,
long after Operation Michael and long
before Mary became a theatre nurse in St Vincent's
and before she met Michael's and May's youngest
Gerry of Castledaly, of St Thomas' GAA club, the man who in pretence

feigned a nosebleed (among other things, like his ability
to golf, to tennis, to croquet;
though in the end betrayed by a hurler's grip on the mallet,
club, and racket,
much to the disdain of haughty Trev)
for her attention, in a lowly impulse, in Dublin's Metropole Dance Hall
while he trained to divvy
up the law at Blackhall

the other side of the Anna Liffey
where life loves an *out-of-reach horizon*,
like the Mexican horizon that was shifty
and became American
after the San Patricios fared quite unquietly unwell
in Churubusco, and Mexico's north
became New. The famine bells
still knelled as the States of Aye-Aye girthed

the New M., and Mexicans (*ad hoc*)
were (legally) made white so they could set and cast

a vote legally. And yes, the cuckoo
has been the state's
statutory bird, the Greater Roadrunner
running out of road in Gila Park
where owls hoot-hoot and cars are eating road (as my father
would say, ar dheis dé…) as if to burke

the desire to leave Truth or Consequences NM hurriedly.
Awe-stroked now I am by the May sun
(…go raibh a anam dílis) on a day fit fairly
for pearling as I move along
west, circumventing Rockefeller Center
and past the Mayfair Hotel, and in a moment of amnesia
I had forgotten 'Love's Labour's
Lost' was in my satchel. So I sit for a slice of pizza

and in a stroke of good luck (and god bless)
I overcame my geyser-like whooping cough
when I was in nappies,
when my mother herself
was studying at Blackhall and my father
(T; god rest him) felt he was in *terra nullius*
with my brother and me. But he soldiered
on through it when spondulicks were scarce. He would soon-after marry

and make her an island of a widow from a stroke he had in a hospital
(Merlin Park – not né-d after King Arthur's legend),
a place designed to cope with an outbreak of Tubercul-
osis (or not to be) where Gerry, his son, and other daughter reckoned
with TB, where two of the three
continued on (and continue to continue) with life
and one of those two briefly
dabbled in a twelve-stepper while his wife

took to the Book. I'm self-conscious
of my wallet now, of a twelve-stepper
chip that impresses
a ring much too like a latex Durex rubber
so I pay with the fiver in one of my satchel's many pockets
on this, the fairest of May days, for there is not a cloud
for there to be any tumult to keep balance
within, much to the delighting lonely impulse of these crowds.

Paul Muldoon's formal ingenuity and mastery of nuanced poetic tropes all buoy the paradoxes of Irish history to the page's surface, among other things. Living in the US the past number of years, his poetry has taken on a new significance for me in coming to terms with the sense of inbetweenness that comes with emigration. While rooted in Yeats' 'An Irish Airman Foresees his Death', the inspiration for my poem comes from Muldoon's Pulitzer Prize-winning collection *Moy Sand and Gravel*: 'At the Sign of the Black Horse, September 1999' wedges itself into and dismantles the confines of another Yeats poem – 'A Prayer for my Daughter' – while deliberating on his and his partner's respective ancestries with breathtaking scope and control. Like so much of his work, his poem expands and contracts, it looks ahead and looks back, it internalises a fleeting world and externalises the human response to it. Simply, his work is incomparable.

The Spomeniks

Ben Keatinge

No one cares about the Spomeniks,
they are lost, like Tito's spaceships
in a galaxy beyond the Draga valley,
rogue astronomers have maimed
the useless beauty of their moons.

My capsule is migrating where
abandoned stars cross other skies,
it cruises south past Maribor
to circle Temerin, turn at Vukovar,
it glides in revolutions of the past.

Then west to Bosnia I steer my craft
to gaze at Grmeč, wonder at Mostar,
my U.F.O. won't need to travel far
to find the trembling obelisk at Srb
nor wake the drowsing stones of Drvar.

This poem is inspired by my fascination with the built heritage of former Yugoslavia, and especially the *spomeniks* which commemorate the Partisan struggle of World War II (*spomenik* means 'monument' in Serbo-Croat and Slovene). They are abstract sculptures built during the Tito era (1945-1980) but now largely neglected, many beyond repair. They are haunting, beautiful and uncanny, looking forward and back, suggestive of a lost utopia that reverberates still. Representing Yugoslav ideals of 'brotherhood and unity', they were created as modernist artworks to affirm the solidarity between Slovenia, Croatia, Serbia, Bosnia and Herzegovina, North Macedonia, Kosovo and Montenegro, all independent countries that emerged subsequently from the violent break-up of Yugoslavia in the 1990s.

The idea for a poem about redundant sculptures was suggested to me by Richard Murphy's sonnets of Irish monuments in his collection *The Price of Stone*. These sonnets articulate Murphy's sense of his own identity and the structures are his mouthpiece. But the monuments have their own voices and histories too, and speak uneasily of their vulnerabilities. 'Wellington Testimonial', the obelisk in Phoenix Park, offers only a 'clean laconic style', completely inadequate to its status as, in Murphy's words from *In Search of Poetry*, 'a monument isolated in a country and a century that have changed… celebrating things or people that nobody remembers …'. At the ruined 'Friary' at Ross Errilly, 'the rain harps on ruins, plucking lost / Tunes from my structure, which the wind pours through / In jackdaw desecration'. Murphy's buildings are untimely structures, marooned, without a role. Yet Murphy's poems convey the useless beauty of their edifices and, by adapting them for the architecture of his poetry, he revives them, as my poem has attempted to do for the *spomeniks*.

Writing Audio Description at the Ulster Museum

Bebe Ashley

I want to talk you through the time and space of early California.
The brush strokes are confident in the white span of sea foam.
The colours are cold and I am sure the sea wall is seeping.

I am happy in the landscapes I've never seen in person.
It does not matter that this is a window-less room,
Venice Beach is well-lit and I wouldn't want to change my view.

The pigment of the watercolour is easily saturated in the paper.
I am trying to list the most important blues when
I am distracted by something new: a close, but different blue.

A few years before I moved to Belfast, I spent a week at the Seamus Heaney Centre Summer School. It was a fantastic introduction to poetry, and to the city. Here, Emma Must introduced me – for the first time – to ekphrasis: the technique of responding to the diverse and exciting world of art through my own poetry. We spent an afternoon in a workshop at the Ulster Museum, exploring the exhibitions and galleries, taking our own time generating poetic responses. Her feedback was very encouraging and was instrumental in setting me on the path of poetry. I've enjoyed investigating ekphrasis over the past few years with sources ranging from Harry Styles to Line of Duty, pushing the definition of visual art.

After the Summer School, I went to No Alibis bookshop to fill my suitcase with books. I picked up *the future always makes me so thirsty: New Poets from the North of Ireland* to read on the flight back. It closes with Emma's poem 'Belfast Pastoral', which captures a city that I closely identify with. It isn't just the mention of Rowntrees Fruit Pastille lollies, or the Tomb Street post office (because I rarely wait home when parcels are supposed to arrive), but the movement of the poem stays with me even now, years later.

Although my poetic interests have extended beyond ekphrasis to the wider accessibility of the arts, the place in Belfast I linger the longest is still the galleries of Ulster Museum, where I pass my time watching the people and the paintings.

Blouse

Nithy Kasa

Mother had a blouse. It was mauve
with puff-sleeves. Roped shoulders
with pads under. The collar peter pan.
The style of the forties. They stitched Devil's
Ivies on the breasts like purple hearts;
Dark sequinned patterns on a plain torso,
sewn to please. Lines swamping, as if the maker
had something to say. Or may have failed
the first twists seamed, so overran them.
The blouse belonged to my grandmother,
who inherited it at sixteen, from her mother.
Because it did not retain, I bought myself one:
mauve, puff-sleeves. The collar peter pan,
like a riflebird at dance. I altered it, v-necked,
glammed. My scaffolded consciousness,
imitating the hands that came before.
The domes on the cuffs too, were my own doing.
I caught myself, strutting my mother's walk,
first day I had it on. It runs in the family,
women with pretty faces,
warm smiles, curls on their circlets.
The poppies on their skins worn elegantly.

At night, I doffed the blouse, naked —
myself in the mirror, one eye shy,
counting the pleats on my skirt,
a man waiting on my bed.
His bust, like that of my grandfather's.
His tongue poetic, like my father's,
before mother had me.
Crystal pieces passed on,
the star-lights, on my ears.

Fortunate as I have been with mentors, the poem 'Blouse' favours Jean
O'Brien. When I began writing, I found myself neutralising the gender of
the narrator, selecting only the themes that seemed profound, and opting
for stronger words to toughen the poems – having learned that books were
generally more successful when they showed masculinity. Too many times,
I'd heard of female writers who had to alter their names in order to be taken
seriously. I, too, followed suit as I started aiming to get my work published
in magazines.

Jean O'Brien is the opposite. I was surprised when I first encountered
her work. She dared to let her books be female, with titles like *Dangerous
Dresses, Lovely Legs, Merman*. I was taken, not only by the choices of titles
but the images on the covers. Light, colourful, girly – rare for a noted poet.
At first glance, you get this gentle feeling, you presume that it is a woman's
work, that it is a woman speaking. A portfolio not subscribing to the status
quo of the male-dominated industry.

As an emerging female poet, it helps to know poets who are female and
celebrate it. I now find myself letting the voices in me speak freely, regardless
of how they may come, with no oppression. I use words as they come to me,
avoiding heavy editing. I am learning to let poems flow without denying
or filtering out the parts I might have thought to be too feminine before.

English Market, 6pm

Eoin Hegarty

after Dennis O'Driscoll's '9am'

Late shoppers, bags knuckled in both hands.
Faces and shop fronts with their shutters drawn;
voices within full of keys and murmurs.

Vaulted shadows, rafters creaking like stiff joints;
dusted by a tussle, a wing-flap, claws on metal,
before the bellied fall of a pigeon, an airy slide

that sets him on the bowl of the empty fountain,
head bobbing and talking to himself. Newspapers
stretched over the fruit, a selection of monochromes,

greying landscapes that smell of damp; wet drafts
with a hint of orange. Buckets cough and scrape;
restless handles tap brisk diminuendos. Lone voices,

sudsy mops and sparrows. A double-decker sighs
while ice from the fish stalls is flecked with dirt
and glittering scales; shovelled onto trays, amplifying

against sheet metal. *Echo*, chants the paperboy
from outside where exhausts shiver and fume,
tipping along the road, coarse as a day's stubble.

A Roma girl empties a paper cup of coins into her hand;
her dress is black and heavy with November. Beside her
a lock is tested; a final word swinging on its hinges.

Dennis O'Driscoll is a poet I keep returning to. An accomplished civil
servant – who described himself once, in typical self-deprecatory fashion, as
the 'Lord of the Files' – his poetic voice and output, with its spare and wry
observations on contemporary life, are witty, moving and totally engaging.
It is a voice that puts trust in clarity, witness and in his own lived experience.
And these are touchstones I'm continually drawn to as I seek to recalibrate
and refine my own writing.

His sense of witness is evident in his prose piece 'Walking Out' from
The Outnumbered Poet, where he sets out on an evening stroll. Any hint that
this might conjure some sort of escapism is quickly dispelled: 'There is no
scenic route around here. No focal point: no shiny-coated river…all roads
lead to nowhere pretty much.'

And yet, the poet in him continues to describe: 'From all directions
come the shrieks and whoops of children; loud, excitable, irritable teenage
hyperbole. A basketball hoop is strapped to a streetlight. A football is lashed
against the wire mesh…A stray ball cowers under car wheels like an escaped
puppy.'

In this way, his poetry also convinces. As Heaney writes in his moving
preface to *Dear Life*, O'Driscoll is 'a poet of the commuter belt, of the alarm
clock and the evening bus, of the business conference and the office party.
His subject, in Frost's words, was common experience but uncommon in
books.'

In '9am', from *Weather Permitting*, he conjures up a city street on an
average morning, whose silent slumber is broken by the sounds of businesses
opening – keys, delivery vans, shutters rolling up; someone stepping out for
a fag. And where objects come alive: 'The sun-striped awning is goaded /
from its layer by a long pole.' And 'Flowers, bleary-eyed from all night truck
journeys, / revive in cool vases…'

At its very simplest, the poem has what O'Driscoll describes in his review of Douglas Dunn's *Terry Street*, as that 'satisfaction of everyday things observed and encapsulated, pondered and clarified, with economy and sympathy...'

And so, with many of my poems, but especially with 'English Market, 6pm', a close-of-day reckoning of the market in Cork city, I too try to articulate this 'satisfaction of everyday things...with economy and sympathy.'

In the Country

Bern Butler

after Mary O'Malley

In winter, space crowds outside,
pushes shaded faces to my windows,
knocks on my door but no one's there.

In summer, teeming hedgerows
fatten air, trees colour in the windows,
fruit stains glass. And though swaddled

in a tighter place, I still crave countable
slabs, blocks, cranes spilling concrete,
claimed space, familiar nooks, street names.

Behind cracked plaster,
from crumbling yellow brick,
a straggly pink weed declaring itself

from the gable of a house
on Helen Street, is enough
to be getting on with.

I met the poet Mary O'Malley in 2001 in Castlerea Prison, where I was working as an English teacher. She was one of the first writers I brought in under the Writers in Prisons Scheme to do a reading and workshop. I remember being struck by the respect Mary showed to students and her interest in their experiences. I had a quiet interest in writing myself but did not share this information with Mary!

Roll on 2019, by which time I'd made inroads into writing by practicing during the lengthy prison lunch break; writing well enough to be accepted onto the NUI Galway MA in Writing where it transpired Mary was the poetry lecturer. She had not forgotten me or the prison workshop, and I believe this allowed her a keener insight into my writing.

Mary was also familiar with the area of the city I grew up in; a council estate called Shantalla. During the Master's, I wrote several poems based on growing up there and Mary suggested that I build on these to form a first collection. This seemed like an unachievable goal, but I persisted and am currently engaged in this project with continued support from Mary.

I wrote 'In the Country' after Mary's poem 'In the City' in *Playing the Octopus,* a collection in which the poet explores themes of place and identity, rural and urban. Traditionally in poetry, it is the beauty of the countryside which is eulogised: I liked that Mary explored the theme more deeply and, in 'In the City', took the opposite point of view.

I admired how well she captured a city in sharp, striking imagery, simultaneously dangerous and beautiful, and the evident power of her carefully selected words, like *flash* and *slices* for example: 'Knives flash like eels in alleyways / High up a silent jet slices the moon / Looking in windows, guarding our dreams.'

For me, besides originality and powerful imagery, it is the air of ease and lightness of touch in this poet's work which I most admire: Mary O'Malley makes the writing of poetry appear deceptively easy – that is, until one tries!

Welcome to Dyskinesia Land

Oliver Nolan

Dyskinesia is the medical term used to describe the tics and involuntary movements associated with the Parkinson's condition.

9:00 am   Almost comatose
With rigid leaden limb,
I struggle to place a tablet in my mouth.
Then a drink;
Mustn't spill the water.

10:15 am   The tablet works,
Dyskinesia kicks in
And lo I'm in Rugby Winger mode!

Movement, Action
Now take over.
I duck and weave,
     I twist and turn;
Now throw passes,
     Then throw shapes;
Jump and shimmy,
     Glide and swivel;
I take some hits,
     Dodge the hard ones,
But — uh oh — the meds are running low.

12:00 pm   C-O-M-A-T-O-S-E again!
But who cares?
Another pill
And I'm out on the wing
                 Again

As a reader, I have always been in awe of writers. I admire their unfettered imagination, their range and control of language, their ability to create an extensive and credible world. In a way, this worship has acted as an inhibitor. Like any average punter, I couldn't hope to reach their lofty standards.

However, having joined a Writers' Circle, I made a couple of discoveries. While not reaching the literary standards of the writers I admire, I could still write in an interesting and entertaining way. Secondly, I discovered that writing was enjoyable and therapeutic. The physical limitations brought on by my condition did not appear to interfere with the process. On the contrary, I could say that writing allowed me to forget that I had Parkinson's.

At first I avoided writing about the disease, but thought it might be helpful as an insider to share the experience. When I did tackle the subject in a poem, the result had too much of the 'poor me'. I came across the Parkinson's poems of Frank Ormsby while experimenting with lines which were to become 'Welcome to Dyskinesia Land'. I liked his poetry. I liked his vision of poetry: '…accessible poems about recognisably everyday subjects, treated humorously… written in language readily understood but used inventively, but with the odd unexpected flourish' (*Reading Ireland*, Winter 2018). Discovering his humorous approach in the Parkinson's poems validated my less-than-serious description of dyskinesia. Humour disarms the limitations of the condition, and has a medicinal value of its own.

This Summer

Tom Roberts

Taking it easy, shooting the breeze, touching
important places. That's my kind of conversation.

I get the sense it's yours too

in this little guesthouse outside Essen.

I ride the breakfast rush, wipe tables, cover hams
in cling film, before you coast to the other side
of my bar. Our preliminaries ebb and flow, in German

natuerlich. You've a meeting in Cologne. Your son
is my age. You wholesale women's clothes. You lost
your arm a long, long time ago. I suppose that was it,

wasn't it, which really opened us up, like the Great
Steppe linking Europe and Asia. Opened us up
to nine-year olds in tank pits with guns. Opened us up

to ten-year olds in tank tops with stones. Opened us up
to men and women. Opened us up to a pleasant surprise,
like rounding an unknown corner on a weekend walk,

to see

a kaleidoscope of tortoiseshell butterflies.

I love that the texture of Irish life has softened over the last few decades, that space has opened up for new definitions, new influences, new growth. If a person wants the old, hard lines, sure they can find them. But if a person wants, desires, *needs* the meanders, the wynds, the gaps which can provide so much sustenance, they can now head there. My writing mentor, the poet Donny O'Rourke, has encouraged me to seek out these places.

I'm from the top right-hand corner of the island, on the coast beside the Irish Sea. On a good day, you can look out and see Scotland. That's where I now live, in Glasgow. Some might say that city is the Irish imprint in Scotland, and that where I'm from is the Scottish imprint in Ireland. Whatever the mix, it's that ground, that water, Europe and America too, which I love exploring through poetry.

Donny leads by example in caring about poetry but there's a greater lesson which he quietly imparts. *Keep going.* If the day job is troubling you. *Keep going.* Whether you're at the peak or trough of a particular relationship. *Keep going.* If the kids are acting up. *Keep going.* If you're crying. *Keep going.* This quiet, gentle art form needs to be prioritised. *Keep going.*

Bare Bones

Molly Twomey

for Leanne O'Sullivan

It's 3:04 p.m. and I'm at Limerick Junction, carrying a rucksack full of steamed veg in Tupperware. My teeth won't stop chattering. I pinch my arms under my leather jacket to warm them. If my mother wasn't here, I'd go for a sprint before the 3:15 train to Galway to burn off the two slices of pineapple that sag in my stomach. My mother hugs me. Her hands linger over the flab at my back, and I am so focused on it that I don't notice her zip down my bag and slip in a copy of *Waiting for My Clothes*.

I run up three floors in Cúirt na Coiribe. My room is as I left it, sheets crumpled on the bed, lycra sweating on a clothes horse. I open my bag and the book falls out – a half-naked woman on the front. I pick it up, flick through. It's a collection of poems about a girl whose flesh eats itself in the cold, who bruises her back doing sit-ups on a rosewood floor, and passes out from making herself vomit. A housemate fries something in the kitchen; the crackle of fat and an eggy stench seep through the walls. I convince myself that somehow the greasy air will slither into my pores and harden to fat. I run and run, down the stairs and over Salmon Weir Bridge. I sprint through Salthill until I can't remember the girl in the poems telling me not to 'look away'[18], and the 'quilted hairs'[19] that grow along her spine.

---

18   Leanne O'Sullivan, 'Perfect Disorder', *Waiting for My Clothes* (Bloodaxe Books, 2004), p. 14.
19   Leanne O'Sullivan, 'Famine', *Waiting for My Clothes* (Bloodaxe Books, 2004), p. 16.

When I'm diagnosed and sent to an eating disorder clinic, I take Leanne O'Sullivan's book with me. I read it and read it and read it again; and think this girl is going through hell. She's demented, bent over the sink with blood dripping down her nose, sticking her fingers down her throat and collapsing onto a scale. I feel sorry for her – she must be exhausted. Doesn't she care about her teeth, the density of her bones? I see her in every patient: in the lanugo on their arms, the dips in their cheeks. I start to write poems about how beautiful they are. I transcribe them in metallic ink on floral pages and slip them under their doors as gifts.

Two years later, I transfer to University College Cork. I admit I'm sick, but now I'm obsessed with eating disorders – writing about them, reading about them, scanning for protruding clavicles and famine eyes in those around me. I memorise whole sections from O'Sullivan's collection and give a presentation on her poem 'Bulimia'. My classmates are subjected to words like amenorrhea, and I blame The Genesis, insisting, "the subject wants to revert to Adam's rib." Dr Flicka Small asks me to stay behind, and I know she's going to recommend counselling. I should have done my project on Maura Laverty, I think. But she smiles, says, "I bought it for you two weeks ago," and hands me O'Sullivan's *Waiting for My Clothes*.

At the end of the year, I'm convinced my dissertation will be on O'Sullivan's first collection, but my supervisor, Alex Davis, isn't as keen. "Have you read Leanne's second collection, *Cailleach: The Hag of Beara?*" he asks. All I know of the Cailleach is that she is a scary old hag and her name means Veiled One, reminding me of a widow who gives out oranges at Halloween. I tell him I'll give it a flick through and google *The Lament of the Hag* from 900 CE. I find a pitiful character who mourns the loss of her beauty and I think she will not inspire me.

I open the book the same hesitant way I arrive at therapy – and I can't believe the things I'm reading. The Cailleach is instinctive and raw, she says and does what she likes, giving the middle finger to anyone who tries to stop her. The first poem I read is 'Sister'[20], where she plans a war for 'after breakfast', and brutally stones her sister to death. She calls her a

20   Leanne O'Sullivan, 'Sister', *Cailleach: The Hag of Beara* (Bloodaxe Books, 2009), p. 15.

'bitch', and a 'cocky thing'. There are no rules, or constraints: she rises from her 'green feast'[21], shakes the pollen from her hair, and uses her 'shape, aged and round'[22] to get what she craves. I speak the words out loud, feeling her vibrancy in my core. I am tired of taking up so little space, of never listening to my needs or hunger. The Cailleach doesn't care about the width of her hips; she is falling in love, giving birth, and shaping the landscape with the rocks gathered in her skirt. I rework my whole thesis and not once do I think of calories or the gym.

On a bench in the rose garden at Fitzgerald's Park, the most important email of my life pings into my phone; I jump, frightening a robin. My cheeks flush and I want to throw myself into the soil, make angels in the earth. I do the next best thing and ring my father: "The School of English just offered me a partial scholarship for an MA," I say. I hear the grin in his voice. For so long, everyone I grew up with has seemed on track to a *proper* career, but now I, too, have some kind of calling, a destiny. I spend the rest of my lunch watching the 'long skies / open like fingers from their dark palms'.[23]

I am in O'Sullivan's class, and she is like Botticelli's Aphrodite with her wavy hair and soothing laugh. She has survived an eating disorder, is about to publish her fourth award-winning collection, and now she is in front of me – ticking my name on a roll and insisting I call her Leanne. I bring her my poems, written during treatment, about rasped bones and fracturing hips. I think she will love these; she will relate so much, she will get me. But she reads them and picks out the vague images, the phrases that jar, the clichéd lines. I've never received this kind of criticism. I'm so used to admiration, but she treats me like anyone else in the room and starts to knock away at the illness I have built my whole life and identity around.

21 Leanne O'Sullivan, 'Hazel', *Cailleach: The Hag of Beara* (Bloodaxe Books, 2009), p. 36.
22 Leanne O'Sullivan, 'Birth Dream', *Cailleach: The Hag of Beara* (Bloodaxe Books, 2009), p. 55.
23 Leanne O'Sullivan, 'Waking', *Waiting for My Clothes* (Bloodaxe Books, 2004), p. 57.

Months later, in Leanne's office, I look out at the silver birches and the students wearing Ray-Bans, rolling cigarettes, and sitting on skateboards. I want to hibernate for the summer, not face a blank page. I wish I were done with this degree; I am so tired of being criticised and never feeling good enough. Leanne snaps me out of it with a book, *Goddesses: Mysteries of the Feminine Divine* by Joseph Campbell. She is bursting off her seat as she tells me about Inanna, Persephone, Ceres – these women who are self-governing, emotional, beautiful, strong. "You must read about them," she insists.

I take the Campbell book to the Lough and feel that buzz in my stomach where every word is fuel – I see Fionnuala in the swans and Arachne in the girl with the dark hair and spidery eyelashes, weaving a scarf. I look down at my legs, see stretchmarks, and I think of all the things that grew when Persephone came back from hell. I write about climate change, the Repeal movement, and sexuality through the voices of Cassandra, Ceres, and Eurydice. My poems go from describing my yearning for bones to thinking about what I can do in the little time I have left in this world.

Now that I have completed my degree and Leanne helps a new group of writers find their strength and voice, her poetry and advice come to me only in my mind. When I find it hard to eat, to go to therapy or to sit still; when the pain returns, too difficult to numb, I recite her poem 'The Cailleach to the Hero'[24] to myself. In it, she reminds me that it isn't enough to exist as a 'mere shadow' or a 'likeness longing to speak'. That I must retrace my steps through the 'road between the living and the dead' and – with every forkful to my lips – feel my 'whole self kicking / and gasping' and fighting to live. That, as she writes, is the real labour. That will be my work.

---

24   Leanne O'Sullivan, 'The Cailleach to the Hero', *A Quarter of an Hour* (Bloodaxe Books, 2018), p. 12.

On Growing Cucumbers

Joanne Kurt-Elli

Remove the male flowers,
the book says,
to avoid bitterness in the fruit.
Six foot three, the vines stretch
the span of the kitchen window.
Tendrils hooked on taut strings
looped over disused curtain rails.
For weeks, I have lived in shadows
of green. Now, the spiked stems
are loaded with wrinkled blossoms
of cadmium, vulgar yellow.
Newly informed, I lift the head of a bloom
examining its anatomy. Gendercidal.
The male flowers grow in clusters,
it tells me. Slender stems, hiding stamens.
Don't confuse them with the pistillate,
those ungainly females
with their thick pedicels –
the immature fruit, which bulges
and engorges and drops its mother flower,
sweetened and seedless
without its male company.
And so poised, fingernails pincered
to decapitate, I notice for the first time
the shape of the leaf. A heart.

Every artist experiences moments of awakening. I remember one of my own such moments: I was on a train, travelling east, dawn was breaking on a winter's morning and I had been gifted a copy of *Waiting for My Clothes*. I remember flicking open the cover and feeling a rush of exhilaration as I started to read. I became so absorbed that I was startled by the announcement of my destination some two hours later. Leanne O'Sullivan's honesty, her incisive articulation, the beauty of her language, and her absolute integrity affected me deeply. That one could be revealing and so utterly without shame opened up a world of writing that I had previously not known to exist.

Her honesty exposed a gaping hole in my own tentative practice. At once, I saw how my preconceptions of what could, or should, form the subject of a poem were based on false premises. I had let my ego outlaw the mining of certain life experiences – too sensitive, too raw, too painful, too intimate – and I had dutifully obeyed. Yet, on that morning, I came to understand that it is in those 'off-limit' zones that the need for greatest exploration lies. Leanne O'Sullivan taught me the ultimate paradox: in rendering oneself vulnerable, in exposing frailty, one becomes unassailable, immune. The very act of articulation transforms pain into beauty, into healing, into clarity. And so, now, as I write, I strive to mine those darker places where my own truth lies.

The Fox

Niamh Twomey

after the poem by Leanne O'Sullivan, with thanks.

A chestnut stain is splayed on the road
at your feet. You eye the dark mining pit
of her empty socket, gouged out by a circling

                  magpie.

Her torn breast is a chamber,
a place to crawl, curl up and sleep
but you are looking to the light, cinders of the day

                  gone by–

You are watching the river tilt in the now-vertical world
of the eye gone from the fox, contemplating its turn.
Or maybe I am reading you wrong. Maybe I am just

                  a hedgerow

arched to the flow of the lane or grass on the verge
cradling stones, sprouting where it's not my business.
Maybe I know nothing of foxes and rivers and

                  souls.

But through blades of green I see you enter,
draw the curtain of bristles on her neck,
find prayer in a fox's gaping wound,

                    glance back,

                                hold open the door–

Leanne O'Sullivan was the Writer-in-Residence at University College Cork when I arrived in Cork as a timid first-year Arts student. English was my favourite subject and I had notebooks full of adolescent scrawls. In a year full of change and a strange new anonymity, I attended her two-hour-long workshops on Wednesday evenings. This quickly became a highlight for me. Leanne was the warmest, most enthusiastic and encouraging teacher I had ever come across, and it was in those workshops that my relationship with poetry began.

Four years later, when I had completed my undergraduate degree, I embarked on an MA in Creative Writing, for which she was the poetry lecturer. She inspired myself and my classmates with her abundance of spirit and boundless love of poetry. I have chosen to write a response to her poem 'The Fox', from her fourth collection, *A Quarter of an Hour*. Without powerful poets such as Leanne, in particular female poets who have paved the way for my generation, I would not be writing poetry.

Seasalted

Elaine Desmond

My grandmother graduated
to New Jersey's glassy, dollared floors

her waterlogged winkle-picked fingers
plunged further, unsalting
bucket by bucket.

Reciting her address by rote,
a poetic tic, seven decades later
Two-Twenty-Two-Lyedecker-Avenue.

Home to a peeled back estuary,
pool-pocked with clamped water
archiving her life to the chimney and me.

Throned in the warmest corner
in our house-favourite flax-green chair,
her endless eye lengthened past walls,
marooned overseas.

She oared miles beyond miles
from island to mainland village,

heard banshee wails flying
between fields

Danced nights beyond nights
and at ninety when I sat by her
feet, facing her words

She bent forward, elbow-creaked
placed her palms over mine
rowed me up from the floor

with her porpoise-blue
tributaried hands
seasalted once more.

I first hear Leanne O'Sullivan reading in Bantry Library at the West Cork Literary Festival in 2018. Her poem 'Note' sifts its way through me for months afterwards. A profoundly beautiful love note which leaves me expanded and glad it exists:

> For I have
> singled you out from the whole world,
> and I would – even as this darkness
> is falling, even when the night comes

Later, I read O'Sullivan's *Cailleach: The Hag of Beara*, where mythology and landscape are never separate and the body resonates with its own nature. I am also of West Cork and hope to scatter the earth and ocean onto words, some day. Like a swimmer's impression in the sea where we feel of-element, we are moulded, fitted into our landscape. Skin to earth-skin, we trace ourselves back to nature via myth.

The following year, I begin a Creative Writing MA at University College Cork, where Leanne O'Sullivan is our poetry teacher. Her classes are charged with a frisson of excitement as she quotes many poems from memory and everything tugs at the heart. We feel our way into some extra-alive place – a whole other way of being where pores are primed to attract some creative frequency.

In early 2020, lockdown becomes a new way of life. We watch army truck convoys in Italy ferrying dead bodies. It is irreversibly sad. We ache for our elders. But poetry eases sorrow. I read Leanne's *Waiting for My Clothes* and am bowled over by 'The Last Rites'. A grandmother's death – the humane beauty of the line, 'I said, You are never leaving.' It stops me up completely and lodges in my throat.

As I write these words, it is still there. Maybe it is never leaving.

Hopewell Place

Scott McKendry

We'd play in the bunker till the weekend
when The Coalman came to spoil our fun.

By then our sooty toys were hid –
The Coalman wasn't just a coalman.

And the man who parked his Polo in the square
and erected a pyramid of Andrex in the boot

was Stewartie, the local black-marketeer,
who'd sell you anything under the sun –

from The Thunderbirds' Tracy Island or a Nintendo
to a bootleg Betamax of *Traci Takes Tokyo*.

And the woman who'd lean over the wall,
into our yard, on Friday nights –

hoping for a favourable northerly wind
to listen in, to hear the latest on The Coalman

as my rum-plied parents spoke out of turn –
was Nosey Norma from next door.

And the man who ran onto The Field in a judogi,
to ask his way home, had fled Flat 10.

And the woman who put cinders in her wheelie bin
burned the kennel and the dog alive.

And on the lane at the end of our row,
where me and Dinsmore threw stones at the soldiers,

two boys hijacked an Electricity Board truck –
with the workman still in the boom lift bucket –

and drove at high speed, till the man fell out
and tumbled onto the bonnet like a gonk troll doll.

This poem, set in north Belfast in the early 1990s, is indebted – like much of what I write – to the fiction of Glenn Patterson. Until I read his *Burning Your Own* (1988) in my late teens, I'd yet to encounter a depiction of Northern working-class Protestant experience that wasn't sodden with cliché. Although that novel, which was Patterson's debut, is set in the late 60s, I recognised ten-year-old Mal Martin, his politically acquiescent family members and his puckish, quasi-mystical mentor Francie Hagan. I knew these people. I, too, had lived amongst the poisonous ideas, insoluble complexities and inhumanity of that conflict we call the 'Troubles'. I, too, had felt loved there, nevertheless.

Burning Your Own gave me permission to portray (and indeed burn, where warranted) *my* own, but it also let me step out of the whole mucky business for a moment to have a think about what I'd been told and shown and what I hadn't – what I knew (that you don't know) and how I might tell you about it. My admiration for Patterson's writing, however, doesn't originate solely from demographic affinity, from some accident of birth. His work walks that tightrope between the parochial and the cosmopolitan (parochi-politan?) – always *cute* where it's didactic, it challenges the tyrannies of stereotypy and documentary realism, broadening the history of the place we call Here. I'd like that from anywhere. It won't come as a huge shock to learn that, years ago, I wrote an undergraduate dissertation on the novels of Glenn Patterson. I sent him it twice and he still hasn't read it. But sure he can read this poem I wrote. It's shorter.

Légende

Leeanne Quinn

(Nano Reid, oil on board)

The remains of the ship can be seen
only at low tide, could a swimmer cut their feet
on the hull's bones if they were to come down
hard from a wave? There's the wave
and then there's the thing that's covered
by the wave. This is what we stare into —
salt stings, blood droplets dissolve into foam.
In July everyone leaves. And I still don't
know if it was the people or the place
I couldn't stand. I was warned not to listen
but it was only a matter of time
before I was cupping my hand to my ear
to see if the sound was real. I looked again
and could make out the whole of the hull
beneath me, then a face and then a face.
I knew then it comes quickly, or not at all.

My father was a publican and proprietor of the Dublin Gate Bar, the pub formerly owned by Nano Reid's family in Drogheda. A mural Nano painted for the bar still adorned the walls when my parents took ownership in the 1970s. Though they sold the bar shortly after I was born, they would often recall her visits. So the name Nano Reid was familiar to me from a very young age. The first painting of hers I saw was brown and muddy with hints of blue. The only recognisable object was the outline of a horse. It was almost as if the painting was buried somewhere in the canvas, the paint trying to obscure the subject. Nano's paintings, and Nano herself, took on mythical qualities for me; her name embedded itself in my mind. Here was an artist who had lived and grown up in my own town, who painted the local landscapes of Drogheda, the environs of Louth and Meath. Nano feels personal. Her paintings are strange and unknowable to me while also being viscerally recognisable. Nano often described her artistic practice in intuitive terms, stating that there was no point in trying to paint a place she had no feeling for. I feel the same way about poetry. The balanced use of abstraction in her work appeals to me. At the same time her work is tangible and grounded in recognisable lore and landscapes. This is all something I carry through to my poetry. From a young age I couldn't look away from Nano's work, and I have been looking ever since.

Exit Strategy with Thyrsi

Sophie Segura

While you puzzle the quantum mechanics of passing
      through walls into sunlight

we warp the graticule, descend on Trianon by proxy,
      hitch our skirts at death and whoop
            your life anthemic.

Should you need it: this bier
            of interconnectedness, a mosh pit of arms
                  to tear at the final integument,

        to ride you sunward, for the silk pad holds fast
                  but the winged thing must out.

With luck, we'll each have a rabble to rend
            and strew us wide. To root, cache marrow,
                  scat our essence to the four winds.

I first encountered Claire Rigby in Buenos Aires, at an ostensibly unsuccessful interview for an administrative assistant position. A journalist and editor, she had an old-school work ethic combined with a teacher's gift for teasing work out of the reticent. I ended up working with Claire as a magazine contributor and, subsequently, subeditor. My lack of formal writing qualifications and experience was irrelevant to her and, as an aspiring writer without a community, I benefitted immeasurably from working alongside her.

We shared our experiences of living between languages and cultures – I grew up in Ireland with a mother from the Gaeltacht and an English father, and as an adult, I've spent many years in the Spanish-speaking world. Conversations with Claire stoked my interest in exploring place and belonging in my poetry.

Witnessing her meticulousness as a writer and editor has served me immensely in my writing. Claire's commitment to feminism and reporting on social justice issues motivated me to continue pursuing similar themes in my own work. Her support, constructive criticism and seize-the-moment attitude encouraged me to persist and to push back against self-doubt regarding my non-academic path to writing.

Claire passed away in 2017, at the age of 45. Generous and altruistic, she inspired loyal, long-standing friendships and had the ability to weave people together both socially and in creative collaboration. It is this that I had in mind when writing 'Exit Strategy with Thyrsi'.

Sacrificial Wind

Liz Quirke

for Lorna Shaughnessy

A night of quiet company, the Town Hall's Studio still
but for the unconscious breaths of strangers
waiting for your Agamemnon to speak his great regret.

Thigh to thigh we cluster in the cheap seats,
and I with no mind yet to touch the Greeks,
invite your lines to blaze ancient worlds to life,

with enough flame to sear the cost of sacrifice, Euripides' lesson
a humming scar on malleable tissue, muscle, heart, memory.
Now our years have laid themselves to rest

and the current swell has gifted us more loss than can be borne.
And what of your Aulis now? What of those left behind
now we know the heavy labour of burying our remembered dead?

Lorna, these are the losings we teach each other – our parents lost
and leaving – acts that you in your quiet way cannot rewrite.
And know I'd rather meet you anywhere but these high winds

Iphigenia was sacrificed to swell. But we are two women-children
mourning the men we've buried, our losses in shards mosaic-small,
dust in winds that decide who shall leave and who shall stay behind.

In 2017, Cúirt International Festival of Literature staged a play written by Lorna Shaughnessy called *The Sacrificial Wind*. The play is comprised of monologues developed from poems in her collection *Anchored*, in which she explores the myth behind Euripides' Iphigenia at Aulis. In the play, Lorna gives voice to all characters from Iphigenia, Agamemnon, Iphigenia's mother Clytemnestra and sisters Electra and Chrysothemis, to a nameless Greek soldier, and playwright Euripides, so that the audience can decide for themselves what has taken place. In her poetry, she explores themes relating to her homeplace of Belfast, family, illness, and in all things, she writes with a clear eye and a true pen. I had known Lorna to see around Galway before I encountered her as a mentor. At a poetry event she approached me when I was struggling to quieten a toddler; eventually she would help me see that my life as a writing mother is one of joy. As my creative PhD supervisor at NUI Galway, she encourages me to cut to the truth in everything and she reads my work with a keen and collegial eye. As individuals, we have had busy, strange, tough years, and even though we're a generation apart, we have both learned from bearing witness to each other's experiences. At the heart of everything, Lorna Shaughnessy is kind, she is real and she is the mentor that I am most fortunate to count in my corner.

Conamara from Dúchruach

Kevin Conroy

Ba dhual don isean a dul chun na mara / *It's a gosling's heritage to go to the sea*

Rocks slighted incessantly by gusts
whispering on their grey heads.

Cogarnaigh mo shinsir
rising with the mist
'ní tír gan teanga'.

Wrinkles on the bog pool –
anáil m'athar, intimations
of nation, language, God

and that playful "You little spriosáin !"

The lilting stream spills sheer
through moss, slamairce and spriosáin,
ag casadh ceol in the wind.

No more cracking ice in Poll an Chapaill.

Fathomed from Léim na hEilte,
   squalls from Cleggan and Clare Island
      quicken the ripples in time
         to crannógs settled on Ballinakill Lake,
            currachs bowing to Manannán's spray,
               family bones uncovered on Omey,
                  cries of the gulls and echoes of clann sinsear at play
                     on Leitergeish strand by the silent sea,
                        to Claddaghduff's Star of the Sea
                           and sagart ár muintire – Fr.Patrick's grave.

Rock
shaped to a headstone, a cornerstone, an altar stone;
the residual scent of incense, my candle's flame
redolent of whispered prayer in my father's land.

My poetry mentor, Peter Sirr, said that one of my early draft poems put him in mind of Pearse Hutchinson's Connemara poems with 'the attention to detail, the use of Irish placenames etc.' He attached Pearse's poem 'Gaeltacht'. I was struck by the image of the tourist taking firewood from the ruins of a boat, and an old man addressing him: 'Aa, a mhac: ná bí ag briseadh báid.' I had a similar experience when considering moving an old abandoned boat into my garden to cover up an unsightly bioCycle wastewater unit.

'Gaeltacht' helped me understand why the property of people who were gone – dead or emigrated – should not be touched. Those abandoned buildings and boats were like relics and somewhat sacred. I revisited my draft with this insight and new respect. And I went on to read more of this poet, broadcaster and translator – champion of cultures that are forced to the edge.

I had five hours of Peter's mentoring from which I gained a mantra and six guiding alerts that I applied in the revised poem 'Conamara from Dúchruach'. They guided me in my first collection of poems that I submitted to the Patrick Kavanagh award, and I was the runner-up that year.

The mantra is drawn from these lines in Wallace Stevens' poem 'Man Carrying Thing': 'The poem must resist the intelligence / Almost successfully.' (I love the 'almost'.)

The alerts are:

1. A big decision in poetry is revealing information at the border between what only you know, and what a reader can be expected to know and relate to.
2. Bring the reader in at the beginning.
3. Poems are not puzzles.
4. Check where your poem seems to become, or to want to become, another poem.
5. Be wary of footnotes.
6. While the best work lives on the edge between the rational and the dreamed, editing is where you decide on the most important thing you want to say.

The Wing-Maker

Paul McMahon

for Matthew

When I finally
decide it's time
to settle up
my life's work
as a wing-maker

I shall leave
the harbour
and walk
the shoreline

that stretches
like a beaten mat
to the headland

whose patchwork
of wheat fields
is the groomed pelt
of a sleeping dog

whose snout sups loam
from the sea

and who,
when the new
moon rises,

shall raise
his rocky head

to rouse
my night-birds out

from their cages,
the many cages –

in the morning
they'll find

a divot of howling,
a broken creel
of fluttering,

my unlaced shoes.

My mentor was the marvellous Matthew Sweeney. He chose me as the recipient for the Words Ireland mentorship award in 2017/18 and for about six months we worked on my debut collection until shortly before the deep loss of his passing. The entire mentorship was a time and an experience that I treasure deeply. I would send him batches of ten to 15 poems and then, a few weeks later, we would meet up and go through them in a room provided by the Munster Literature Centre. I was always anxious as we sat down around the wooden table and Matthew pulled out the poems. I can still hear his voice booming out when he went over a poem – "This poem! When I read it, I said, *this is an important poem*. And then I came to this word..." He glared at me and narrowed his eyes as his forefinger stabbed a word on the page: "This word – I could have hung you for this word." He wasn't joking. And needless to say, he was right. Then he continued onto the next poem and looked at me with sincere joy: "Now this poem! This is playing football for Spain!"

'The Wing-Maker' is a poem that I redrafted after Matthew's many suggestions. When I first presented it to him the poem began: 'When I finally / decide it's time / to settle up / my life's work / I shall...' and Matthew said, "You must say *your life as something...*" When I said, 'My Life as a Painter' of course I was really talking about 'My Life as a Poet'. Then he gave me further suggestions regarding the poem – "Decide on whether or not it is *like a...* or it *is a* groomed pelt. And is it a real or an imaginary dog that raises its head? Whatever you decide – make that the same throughout the poem." The next time we met in the Munster Literature Centre, as I watched Matthew reading the redraft: 'When I finally / decide it's time / to settle up / my life's work / *as a wing-maker...*' an endearing smile beamed across his face.

Committed to instilling in me his own personal DNA for poetry, Matthew went through my entire body of poetry as though it was the only important thing in the world. He had given his entire life to poetry and, even though he knew what was facing him at this time, he told me: "There's no money in poetry, but if I was to live my life again, I would live it exactly the same."

Fruit Flies

Phillip Crymble

Rising from the spoiled late-season peaches
in our wedding bowl — a sudden bloom
of fruit flies like the ones that used to hover
round the trash and philodendrons

in the kitchen of your studio. On Fridays,
with a case of ale, I'd wait out on the porch
for your arrival — see you ambling through
the Old Fourth Ward like Whitman in a field

of summer clover. An onion bag of pears
and wilted tubers in your lap, you'd sit
and smoke a while — debate the early works
of Rothko — bring up "Cirque d'Hiver."

Upstairs in your apartment — the Bartletts cored
and roughly pared — we'd listen to the songs
of Leonard Cohen. The world outside undoing all
its mending — the fruit flies like confetti in the air.

I first contacted Richard Tillinghast while applying to the University of Michigan. I knew he had studied with Robert Lowell and was good friends with Seamus Heaney, but what struck me the most was how accomplished he was as a poet in his own right. Although he often wrote in free verse, Richard's understanding of English prosody was astonishing. I once remember mentioning to him how much I admired William Carlos Williams. Richard replied that the problem with Williams was that his poems had no counterpoint. Over the years, my friendship with Richard has deepened, but I will always value this early lesson. From that time forward, measure, rhythm and musicality have become central to my practice, and 'Fruit Flies' demonstrates my sustained allegiance to Richard's core beliefs and sensibilities.

Throughout the 1990s, Richard taught at the Poets' House in Islandmagee and, for many years, served on its board of directors. Richard's contributions to Irish letters and culture are considerable. In 2008, he published *Finding Ireland: A Poet's Explorations of Irish Literature and Culture*, and in 2009, Dedalus Press published his *Selected Poems*. He has also lived in both Kinvara and Tipperary. My own ties to Ireland are substantial as I was born and raised in Ulster. Over the course of my career, I have published widely in Irish journals and one of my greatest honours was to have a poem selected to appear in *Poetry Ireland Review* under the editorship of former Ireland Professor of Poetry Eiléan Ní Chuilleanáin.

Contributors

Kate Caoimhe Arthur was born in Bangor, Co. Down in 1979, and lives now in the Cambridgeshire Fens with her family. In 2017, she became the Fenland Poet Laureate. In 2018, she was selected for the Poetry Ireland Introductions series. Her work has been published in *The Fenland Reed*, *The Tangerine* and *Best British and Irish Poetry* 2018. She works in collaboration with the fine art printmaker Iona Howard and is working on a pamphlet of Fen-based poems.

Bebe Ashley lives in Belfast. She is an AHRC funded PhD candidate at the Seamus Heaney Centre for Poetry. Her poetry can be found, most recently, in *Poetry Birmingham Literary Journal*, *Poetry Ireland Review*, *Banshee*, *Modern Poetry in Translation*, *Poetry Jukebox* and *The Tangerine*. Her debut collection, *Gold Light Shining*, was published with Banshee Press in Autumn 2020. Bebe has received support from the Arts Council of Northern Ireland to transcribe *Gold Light Shining* into Braille.

Bern Butler is a Galway-based writer and teacher. Her work has featured in *Force 10*, *Ropes Anthology*, *The Galway Review*, *Vox Galvia*, *North West Words*, *The Blue Nib*, *Pandemic.ie* and *Abridged* 0-60. She holds an MA in Writing from NUI Galway, and was a featured reader in Galway City Library's *Over the Edge* Readings. She works in Adult Education and spent 24 years working in prison education.

Kevin Cahill is a poet from Ireland. He has completed a debut collection of poems, and is presently seeking a publisher. To date, his work has appeared in magazines in Ireland and abroad including *The Stinging Fly*, *Southword*, *Crannóg*, *The Manchester Review* and *Magma*.

Conor Cleary is from Tralee and lives in Belfast where he is studying toward a PhD. His work has appeared in *The Tangerine*, *Poetry Ireland Review*, *The Stinging Fly* and *Virginia Quarterly Review*. In 2018, he was the winner of the Patrick Kavanagh Poetry Award. His debut poetry pamphlet, *priced out*, was published by The Emma Press in 2019.

Kevin Conroy's work has been published in *The Irish Times*, *The Stony Thursday Book*, *One* by jacar press, *The Moth*, *THE SHOp*, *Southword*, *Burning Bush II*, *Boyne Berries*, *The Blue Max Review*, *The Curlew*, *Sixteen Literary Magazine*, *erbacce*, *The Runt magazine*, and *Skylight 47*. His poems have been shortlisted/longlisted in competitions such as the Fish Poetry Prize, Fool for Poetry Chapbook Award, Algebra of Owls, and published in anthologies including *Poets Meet Politics* and *Hibernian Writers*. He was a runner-up in The Patrick Kavanagh Poetry Awards 2016.

Phillip Crymble is a physically disabled writer and literary scholar living in Atlantic Canada. A poetry editor at *The Fiddlehead*, he holds an MFA from the University of Michigan and has published poems in *Oxford Poetry*, *Magma*, *The North*, *The Stinging Fly*, *Poetry Ireland Review*, *The Forward Book of Poetry* (2017), and elsewhere. In 2007, he was invited to participate in Poetry Ireland's Introductions series in Dublin. In 2015, *Not Even Laughter*, his first full-length collection, was released by Salmon Poetry.

Jerm Curtin is from Co. Cork, but lives in Spain. His poems have won a number of prizes, including the Writers' Week Single Poem Competition on two occasions. He was one of the runners-up in the 2019 Patrick Kavanagh Award.

Monica De Bhailís is a native of Wexford and a University College Dublin graduate, now living in Dublin. Recently retired from her career as a civil servant, she now works part-time for a number of NGOs. She is also working on a study of the Bronte sisters' Irish links and influences.

Stephen de Búrca lives in Gainesville, Florida where he earned his poetry MFA from the University of Florida in 2020. From Galway City, Stephen won the poetry award for the *Over the Edge* New Writer of the Year 2019 prize. His poetry has appeared or is forthcoming in *Poetry Ireland Review, Fish Anthology* 2019, *Crannóg, Southword, Skylight* 47, *The Honest Ulsterman, Boyne Berries,* and *Abridged.*

Helen Dempsey from Rush, Co. Dublin has had poems published in anthologies, magazines, online, local radio, poetry readings and open mic sessions. She won Fingal Libraries' Poetry Day competition 2018, a commended and highly commended award in the Jonathan Swift Poetry Competition 2017, and was shortlisted for the Bridport Prize in 2018. A member of the Ardgillan Creative Writers' Group, she holds a Masters in Poetry Studies from Mater Dei College, Dublin City University and is working towards her first collection.

Elaine Desmond lives in West Cork where she eavesdrops on curlews and herons. Her poems have appeared in *Cathexis Northwest Press, The Ogham Stone, Fresher,* and *Cork Words.* She was shortlisted for the Fish Poetry Prize 2019. She is a part-time student of the Creative Writing MA at University College Cork.

Marguerite Doyle is a poet and writer from Dublin who is interested in her native city and its environs as the poetic space. She graduated from Dublin City University in 2020 with an MA in Creative Writing. Marguerite received a special mention for her entry to the Desmond O'Grady International Poetry Prize 2020. Her work was shortlisted in the *A3 Review*'s Monthly Poetry Competition. She received first runner-up and was highly commended by the *Anthology Magazine*'s Short Story Prize 2020. Marguerite's work appears in DCU's *The College View, Visions*

International: The World Journal of Illustrated Poetry, Third Wednesday, Snakeskin, Automatic Pilot, Vallum: Contemporary Poetry and *Vita Brevis Press*. Marguerite is a full-time family carer.

Rory Duffy has had work published in several journals including *Southword, Crannog, The Stony Thursday Book, A New Ulster, Skylight 47, Boyne Berries* & *The Cormorant*. In 2019 he won the Red Line Book Festival (Poetry) Prize and came second in the Strokestown Summer Poetry Award. Rory's short stories have been shortlisted/highly commended in many competitions as well as being broadcast on RTÉ.

Tim Dwyer's chapbook is entitled *Smithy of our Longings: Poems From The Irish Diaspora* (Lapwing Publications). He has been published in many literary journals including *Cyphers, Poetry Ireland Review*, and *The Stinging Fly*. He was born in Brooklyn and his parents were from Galway. Prior to retirement, he was a psychologist at a women's correctional facility in New York. Recently moved from the United States, he now makes his home in Bangor, County Down.

Roan Ellis-O'Neill is a poet from Belfast. He received his BA in English Literature at Macalester College, Minnesota, where he researched the intersections of poetry, ethnography, and histories of violence. In 2018, Roan was the recipient of a Mellon Foundation Lifelong Learners Collaborative Research Grant. His first article, co-authored with Professor Amy E. Elkins, is forthcoming from *Interdisciplinary Literary Studies* titled 'Uncovering Jean McConville: Seamus Heaney's Poetic Cartography of the Disappeared.'

Orla Fay edits *Boyne Berries*. Recent work has appeared in *Poetry Ireland Review, Impossible Archetype, Crannóg* and *The Lake*. She won 3rd place in The Oliver Goldsmith Poetry Competition 2019 and was shortlisted in The Cúirt New Writing Prize 2019. She was highly commended in The Francis Ledwidge Poetry Award 2019. Her poem, 'The Natural Order', was published as poem of the week in *The Irish Times* in July 2019. Her debut collection, *Word Skin*, is forthcoming from Salmon Poetry.

Peter Frankman is an American through and through. He was born in the Midwest and grew up across the States, living everywhere from Georgia to California. He received his BA in English and Journalism/Mass Communications from the University of Iowa where he studied under Mark Mayer and Venise Berry. He is a recent graduate of the MPhil in Creative Writing from Trinity College Dublin.

Sonya Gildea is a 2020 winner of the Ireland Chair of Poetry Student Award and winner of the Cúirt International New Writer's Award 2015. She has been published in *Crannóg*, *The Stinging Fly* and *The Irish Times*. Sonya completed an MA in Creative Writing at University College Dublin in 2020. She lives and works in Dublin, Ireland, and is completing the chapbook *The Nine River Beats of Owenea*, and is developing the book-length poem and installation *Rewriting the Constitution*.

Jackie Gorman is a graduate of the Irish Centre for Poetry Studies at Dublin City University. Her work has been published in journals such as *Poetry Ireland Review*, *The Lonely Crowd* and *The Honest Ulsterman*. In 2017, she was selected for the Poetry Ireland Introductions Series and received the Listowel Writers' Week Single Poem Award. She has also been commended in the Bord Gáis Energy Irish Book Awards and the Patrick Kavanagh Poetry Award. Her debut collection was published by The Onslaught Press in 2019.

Lynn Harding is an editor from Cork, living and working in Dublin. Her poetry has been published in *Poetry Ireland Review*, *The Irish Times* and the *Poetry Birmingham Literary Journal*. She has been featured on Dublin South FM's 'Rhyme and Reason' radio arts programme, and has performed across Ireland and Northern Ireland, including at the Cork International Poetry Festival.

Jake Hawkey was born in London, studied Fine Art at the University of Westminster, and is currently studying for an MA in Poetry at the Seamus Heaney Centre, Queen's University Belfast. His poems have been published by *Live Canon*, *The Honest Ulsterman* and anthologised in the *Best New British And Irish Poets* 2019-2020 (Eyewear, UK). Jake was recently the inaugural intern at The River Mill Writers' Retreat, Downpatrick.

Eoin Hegarty is a primary school teacher based in Midleton, Co Cork. In 2018, he won the Cúirt New Writing Prize, and was shortlisted for the Poetry Collection Award in the Listowel Writers' Competition. In 2019, he participated in a mentorship programme with American poet Sandra Beasley, and was invited to read at the Poetry Introductions Series during the Cork International Poetry Festival. His poems have been published in *Poetry Ireland Review*, *The North* and *Southword*. He was selected for the Poetry Ireland Introductions Series 2020.

Emily Holt is the author of *Though the Walls Are Lit* (Lost Horse Press, 2020). She received a Master of Letters in Literature from Trinity College Dublin and an MFA in Creative Writing from the Rainier Writing Workshop at Pacific Lutheran University. Her poems and essays have appeared in *Poetry Ireland Review*, *Hinterland*, and other publications. She lives in Seattle, Washington.

Nithy Kasa is a poet from DR Congo. She was a guest poet for Carlow University's MFA Residency 2019, and was shortlisted for the Red Line Book Festival the same year. She has read for Poetry Ireland, RTÉ Poetry Programme, and the Royal Irish Academy. Her work appears in *Writing Home: The 'New Irish' Poets* (Dedalus Press, 2019), *A New Ulster*, Dublin Business School's archive as well as the National University of Ireland Galway's archive, and elsewhere.

Ben Keatinge is a Visiting Research Fellow at the School of English, Trinity College Dublin. His poems have been published in *Irish Pages*, *The Stony Thursday Book*, *Orbis*, *Eborakon*, *The Galway Review*, *Agenda*, *Cassandra Voices*, *Flare* and in *Writing Home: The 'New Irish' Poets* (Dedalus Press, 2019). He taught English literature for nine years at South East European University, North Macedonia and he has travelled widely in the Balkans. He is the editor of *Making Integral: Critical Essays on Richard Murphy* (Cork University Press, 2019).

Ruth Kelly is based at the Centre for Applied Human Rights at the University of York. Her research looks at how storytelling and other cultural practices can help activists re-imagine development and human rights. She herself is Irish, and she is working with artists and activists from Bangladesh, Uganda and the UK.

Sven Kretzschmar is from Germany. His poetry has been published widely including with the *Poetry Jukebox*, *Writing Home: The 'New Irish' Poets* (Dedalus Press, 2019) and *Turangalîla-Palestine* (Dairbhre). He was the winner of the 'Creating a Buzz in Strokestown' competition, and his work has been shortlisted and/or received special mentions for several awards and competitions in 2019 and 2020. He has studied in Ireland, worked for Irish Studies organisations, and is a volunteer for German-Irish Society Saarland.

Joanne Kurt-Elli is from Athlone, Co. Westmeath. A former solicitor, she has returned to Ireland after living abroad for twenty years and is a recent graduate of the MPhil in Creative Writing from Trinity College Dublin. An emerging poet and short story writer, her work has previously appeared under the name of CJ Flynn in HCE Review.

Aoife Lyall was awarded an Emerging Scottish Writer residency by Cove Park in 2020 and twice shortlisted for the Hennessy New Writing Awards. Her poems have appeared in *Butcher's Dog*, *Acumen*, *Magma*, *The Stinging Fly*, *Banshee*, *Under the Radar*, *Poetry Ireland Review*, *The Irish Times* and *Gutter*, among others, and are forthcoming in *New Writing Scotland #38* and *Staying Human: new poems for Staying Alive* (Bloodaxe Books). Her debut collection *Mother, Nature* will be published by Bloodaxe Books in 2021.

Joanne McCarthy writes in Waterford, in both English and Irish. She is most recently published in *Boyne Berries* and *The Honest Ulsterman* and has work forthcoming in the *Stony Thursday Book* and *The Stinging Fly*. She is founder and co-editor of *The Waxed Lemon*. Tweets @josieannarua

Peggy McCarthy is currently completing the MA in Creative Writing at University College Cork. She won the Fish Poetry Prize 2020. She has been shortlisted for the Wells Open Poetry Competition 2020. She worked as a primary teacher for many years. Born near Skibbereen in West Cork, Waterford city has been home since childhood.

Scott McKendry is a recent doctoral graduate from Queen's University Belfast, and the recipient of the 2019 Patrick Kavanagh Award. His debut pamphlet, *Curfuffle* (The Lifeboat, 2019), was selected as the Poetry Book Society's 2019 Autumn Pamphlet Choice. His poems have been published in *Virginia Quarterly Review*, *The Poetry Review*, *Magma*, *The Tangerine*, *Public Illumination Magazine*, *The Manchester Review*, *Cyphers*, *The North*, *Poetry Ireland Review*, *The Dark Horse*, *The French Literary Review* and *Poetry London*.

Paul McMahon is originally from Belfast, and lives in Cork. His debut poetry chapbook, *Bourdon*, is published by Southword. Poetry awards include 1ˢᵗ prize in The Keats-Shelley, The Moth International, The Nottingham Open, The Westival, The Golden Pen, and 2ⁿᵈ prize in The Basil Bunting and The Salt International. His poetry has appeared in *The Poetry Review*, *The Threepenny Review*, *The North*, *The Stinging Fly*, *Poetry Ireland Review*, *Agenda*, *The Irish Times*, *The Best New British and Irish Poets*, and elsewhere.

Julie Morrissy is a poet, academic, critic, and activist. Her debut collection *Where, the Mile End* is published by Book*hug (Canada) & tall-lighthouse (UK). She is the inaugural John Pollard Newman Fellow in Creativity at University College Dublin. Her poetry has been published internationally, including in *The Manchester Review*, *The Irish Times*, *bath magg*, *Winter Papers*, and *Poetry Ireland Review*. She is a recipient of the 'Next Generation' Award from The Arts Council. Her website is www.juliemorrissy.com

Emma Must lives in Belfast. Her poem 'Toll' won the inaugural Environmental Defenders Prize at the Ginkgo Awards in November 2019. In 2018 she received an Arts Council of Northern Ireland ACES award. Her poems appear in *Writing Home: The 'New Irish' Poets* (2019), *The Best New British and Irish Poets* (2017), and *New Poets from the North of Ireland* (2016). Her debut poetry pamphlet, *Notes on the Use of the Austrian Scythe* (2015), won the Templar Portfolio Award.

Chandrika Narayanan-Mohan is a Dublin-based arts manager and writer from India. Her work has been aired on NPR and Irish radio, and she regularly performs at events in Ireland. She was an Irish Writers Centre XBorders participant in 2018 and 2020. Her work has been published in *Writing Home: The 'New Irish' Poets* (Dedalus Press, 2019), and, most recently, in *The Honest Ulsterman*. She is currently guest editor of Poetry Ireland's *Trumpet* pamphlet, and a book reviewer for Children's Books Ireland's *Inis* magazine.

Oliver Nolan was born in Westmeath. He went to school at Belcamp in North Dublin before studying in University College Dublin. He married an Artane girl and "landed her in the middle of a beet field in Tipperary" (her words). He taught English in Cashel until 2005. The family returned to Northside Dublin in 2017 and Oliver regards his joining the writers' group in Donaghmede Library as one of his better decisions.

Kelly O'Brien is from Dublin. She completed her degree in English Studies in Trinity College Dublin, and recently graduated with an MA in Poetry from Queen's University Belfast.

David Morgan O'Connor writes and translates from Portugal. He has an MFA from both University College Dublin and University of New Mexico, plus a Masters in Text and Performance from The Royal Academy of Dramatic Art. He is a contributing reviewer for Rhino Poetry and fiction editor at Bending Genres. His work has appeared in *Splonk, A New Ulster,*

Dodging the Rain, Cormorant, Crannóg, Opossum, The New Quarterly, The Guardian, The Irish Independent among others.

Art Ó Súilleabháin was born in Corr na Móna, Co. Galway and spent some years in Boston, USA. He worked in Dublin, Castlebar and Washington DC before returning to Corr na Móna. He won the Aurivo/North West Words Poetry Competition in 2018, and his work has been featured in *Poetry Ireland Review, Boyne Berries, Skylight 47, Salt on the Coals* (Winchester) and with Cinnamon Press. He has published books for children and has read on Sunday Miscellany in English and Irish.

Leeanne Quinn was born in Drogheda and grew up there and in Monasterboice, Co. Louth. Her debut collection, *Before You*, was published by Dedalus Press in 2012, and was highly commended in the Forward Prize for Poetry 2013. Her poems have been widely anthologised, appearing in *The Forward Book of Poetry* 2013, and *Windharp: Poems of Ireland Since* 1916, among others. Her second collection, *Some Lives*, was published by Dedalus Press in October 2020. She lives in Munich, Germany.

Liz Quirke is a poet and scholar from Kerry who has been in Galway for the last ten years. She teaches on the MA in Writing at NUI Galway where she is researching a practice-based PhD on representations of queer kinship in contemporary poetry. Salmon Poetry published her debut collection *The Road, Slowly* in 2018 with her second collection *How We Arrive in Winter* to follow at the end of 2020.

John James Reid is a poet and an architect. Published pamphlets include *Mid-Atlantic, The Goalkeeper,* and *After Six Weeks*. Poems appear in *Clover - A Literary Rag, Nashville Review,* and *Ekphrastic Review*. He was awarded an Irish Writers Centre bursary to attend the W. B. Yeats Summer School, and was also selected to attend the Seamus Heaney Poetry Summer School, in 2018 and 2019. He is currently completing an MA in Poetry at Queen's University Belfast.

Matthew Rice was born in Belfast. Poems have appeared in *Poetry Ireland Review*, *Ashville Poetry Review*, *The Dark Horse*, *The Tangerine*, and in *The Best New British and Irish Poets* 2017. He was the runner-up for the Seamus Heaney Award for New Writing 2017, and was selected for the Poetry Ireland Introductions Series the same year. He is studying on the MA in Poetry at Queen's University, Belfast. His debut collection is due in April 2021 with Summer Palace Press.

Connie Roberts, a County Offaly native, is the author of *Little Witness* (Arlen House, 2015), a collection of poetry inspired by her experiences growing up in an industrial school in the Irish midlands. The collection was shortlisted for the Shine/Strong Award. She is a recipient of the Patrick Kavanagh Award and the Listowel Writers' Week Poetry Collection Award. She was selected as the Exceptional Offaly Person of the Year 2016. She teaches creative writing at Hofstra University, New York. Website: https://connierobertspoet.com

Tom Roberts is writing poetry again after a respite of several years. He's from County Antrim. His poetry and reviews have been published in *London Grip* and in several anthologies, including those on conflict and which showcase Glasgow-based poets. He's a solicitor specialising in EU, public and consumer law with a keen interest in languages. He was an Erasmus student in Germany and worked for several years in Brussels.

Sophie Segura is from Dublin. She holds a degree in Archaeology and Greek and Roman Civilisation from University College Dublin, and has worked as an editor and clothing designer, among other things. Her poetry has featured in Irish and international publications including *Magma*, *The Rumpus*, *Banshee*, *American Poetry Journal*, and *About Place Journal*. She has also written (as Sophie Parker) for *The Irish Times* and *Time Out Buenos Aires*. She has two young children and currently lives between Madrid and Buenos Aires.

Evgeny Shtorn is a writer, activist and researcher from St. Petersburg. In 2018, he was forced to leave Russia; in 2019, he was granted international protection in the Republic of Ireland. His poems have been published in academic journals, anthologies and new media outlets in Russia, Spain, Germany, and Ireland. In 2020, he received the GALAs Person of the Year Award from the National LGBT Federation of Ireland. He is currently working on his first collection, *Translating from Myself*.

James Stafford holds an MA in Creative Writing from University College Dublin. He has been a regular participant in writing workshops facilitated by Yvonne Cullen, and he is researching and beginning to write about authorship and intertextuality.

Molly Twomey holds an MA in Creative Writing from University College Cork and has been published by *Poetry Ireland, Banshee, The Irish Times, Crannóg*, educate.ie and elsewhere. She won the Waterford Poetry Prize in 2020, Padraic Colum Poetry Prize in 2019, and was shortlisted for Over the Edge's New Writer of the Year Award in 2018 and 2019. Selected for Words Ireland's National Mentoring Programme 2020, she is currently under the guidance of Grace Wells.

Niamh Twomey is a poet from County Clare. Her poetry has been published in various journals and anthologies, most recently *Boyne Berries* and the 2 *Meter Review Anthology* (2020). She holds a BA in English and French and an MA in Creative Writing, both from University College Cork, where she began writing poetry under the mentorship of Leanne O'Sullivan.

Benjamin Webb is a poet from Castlerock, Co. Derry. He is going into his final year studying Anglo-Saxon, Norse and Celtic at the University of Cambridge, during which he intends to focus on Medieval Irish Literature and Celtic Philology. He is currently co-editor of *The Dodo*, his college's literary magazine, and his work has recently been published in *The Mays Anthology*.

Milena Williamson is currently pursuing a PhD in Creative Writing at the Seamus Heaney Centre at Queen's University Belfast. She was the winner of the Mairtín Crawford Poetry Award in 2018. Her poetry has been published on RTÉ and in *The Tangerine, Poetry Ireland Review, Poetry Birmingham Literary Journal,* and *Blackbox Manifold* among others. Find more of her work at www.milenawilliamson.com

In Gratitude

We would like to express our deepest gratitude to Eiléan Ní Chuilleanáin, for believing in us and bringing us together; Maureen Kennelly, for giving us wings; Eoin Rogers: conspirator, saviour, friend; Noelle Moran, for your dedication to seeing this book through; Lucy Collins and Philip Coleman, for sharing your insight and experience; Stephen Sexton: wise wizard and guide; and Frank Ormsby, for your generous engagement and guidance.

We are indebted to everyone at The Ireland Chair of Poetry Trust, Poetry Ireland, UCD Press, The Arts Council of Ireland, Arts Council of Northern Ireland, Trinity College Dublin, University College Dublin, and Queen's University Belfast, for their support in making this project possible.

MM: 'Tentative as he was, it might have meant happiness.' – Marilynne Robinson

SM: 'I was no one, and the peace felt huge inside me' – Harry Clifton

MP: 'love grows by what it remembers of love.' – Lisel Mueller

NZ: 'Ah, that was it, the truth at last. Everything would have been love.' – Iris Murdoch

Acknowledgements

The editors, authors, and the publisher gratefully acknowledge the following for permission to reprint copyrighted material. Every effort has been made to seek copyright clearance on referenced text. If there are any omissions, UCD Press will be pleased to insert the appropriate acknowledgement in any subsequent printing or editions.

Miroslav Holub: 'The door', translated by Ian Milner, from *Poems Before & After: Collected English translations* (Bloodaxe Books, 2006). Reprinted by kind permission of Bloodaxe Books.

Paula Meehan: 'The Child I Was', and 'The Commemorations Take Our Minds Off the Now', from *Geomantic* (Dedalus Press, 2016). Reprinted by kind permission of Dedalus Press.

Noel Monahan: 'Advice to a Young Poet', published in *The Irish Times* (March 14, 2020). Reprinted by kind permission of *The Irish Times*.

Selected Bibliography

Jean Bleakney: 'Fenestration', from *Ions* (Lagan Press, 2011).

Nuala Ní Dhomhnaill: 'Titim i nGrá', translated by Paul Muldoon, from *The Astrakhan Cloak* (The Gallery Press, 1992).

Galina Gamper: 'Chto is togo, chto lestnitsa kruta', quoted excerpt translated from the original Russian by Evgeny Shtorn (Zhurnal 'Neva', 2003).

Paula Meehan: 'The Beauty (Of It)', from *Geomantic* (Dedalus Press, 2016); and 'Chapman Lake: Still Life with Bomber', from *Reading the Sky* (Beaver Row Press, 1985).

Richard Murphy: *In Search of Poetry* (Clutag Press, 2017); and *The Price of Stone* (Faber & Faber, 1985).

Dennis O'Driscoll: 'Walking Out', from *The Outnumbered Poet: Critical Essays and Autobiographical Prose* (The Gallery Press, 2013); and '9am', from *Weather Permitting* (Carcanet Press, 1999).

Mary O'Malley: 'In the City', from *Playing the Octopus* (Carcanet Press, 2016).

Leanne O'Sullivan: 'Note', and 'The Cailleach to the Hero', from *A Quarter of an Hour* (Bloodaxe Books, 2018).